CHRISTMAS STOCKINGS

18 HOLIDAY TREASURES TO KNIT

Interweave Press

Editorial Director: Marilyn Murphy
Editor: Elaine Lipson
Technical Editor: Jean Lampe
Copy Editor: Nancy Arndt
Cover Design: Bren Frisch

Designer: Dean Howes
Photo Styling: Susan Strawn Bailey
Photography: Joe Coca
Illustrations: Gayle Ford,
Susan Strawn Bailey

Acknowledgements

The editor would like to extend special thanks to Marilyn Murphy and Linda Ligon at Interweave Press for encouragement, creativity and support, and to all the wonderful designers whose talent and enthusiasm made this collection a pleasure to put together. Thanks also to Jean Lampe for her meticulous and patient technical editing and good humor, to Dean Howes for creative and graceful book design, to photographer Joe Coca and photo stylist Susan Strawn Bailey, and to everyone on the Interweave team.

Interweave Press
201 East Fourth Street
Loveland, CO 80537 USA
www.interweave.com

Printed in Hong Kong

Library of Congress Cataloging-in-Publication Data

Christmas Stockings: 18 Holiday treasures to knit / [editor, Elaine Lipson].
p. cm.
ISBN 1-931499-00-4
1. Knitting-Patterns. 2. Christmas stockings. I. Lipson, Elaine, 1957-II. Interweave Press.
TT825 .C396 2001
746.43'2041—dc21

2001024996

10 9 8 7 6 5 4

CONTENTS

Introduction 4
How to Use this Book 4
Abbreviations and Glossary of Techniques 5

18 Christmas Stockings to Knit

Easy to Intermediate Designs

Snowy Night Gansey Stocking, by Lisa Carnahan 10
Christmas Rainbow Surprise, by Barbara Albright 13
Sock Monkey Stocking, by Linda Ligon 16
The Chubby Sock, by Lynn Gates 19
Paintbox Pocket Stocking, by Barbara Albright 22
The Big Easy, by Tara Jon Manning 26
Keepsake Baby Stocking, by Jennifer Carpenter 29
Giant Jester Stocking, by Sandy Cushman 33
Snowman at Midnight, by Nicky Epstein 36

Intermediate to Advanced Designs

Diamonds in the Rough Argyle Stocking, by Jennifer Steinberg 40
Village of Kirbla Estonian Stocking, by Nancy Bush 44
A Fetching Stocking, by Kathy Brklacich Sasser 48
Counterpane and Lace Stocking, by Susan Strawn Bailey 52
Hugs and Kisses Aran Stocking, by Dee Lockwood 57
Naughty but Nice Victorian Elegance, by Sasha Kagan 63
Scandinavian Stocking, by Donna Kay 67
Celtic Christmas Fair Isle Stocking, by Ron Schweitzer 71
Austrian Alpine Treasure, by Candace Eisner-Strick 75

Miniature Mittens and Stocking Ornaments 83
Design Your Own:
Basic Stocking Patterns for Sport/Double Knitting Weight, Worsted Weight, and Bulky Weight Yarns 87
Alphabet Chart 94
Yarns 95
Yarn Suppliers 96

INTRODUCTION

The Christmas stocking tradition, it's said, began with the daily task of hanging socks by the fire to dry on winter nights, centuries before clothes dryers and central heating. As Santa came down one fated chimney on Christmas Eve, the story goes, gold coins spilled from Santa's pockets into the socks. When the coins were discovered by the socks' young owners, word spread—and the charming custom of hanging "Christmas stockings" to be filled with small treasures and gifts began.

Naturally, it wasn't long before knitters began making special stockings that were not only decorative, but held lots of stuff. Knitters have always loved making socks, and many jumped at the chance to make extra-large versions with room for lush patterning, color, personalization, and creativity. Christmas stockings also proved an ideal format to combine regional knitting styles with holiday spirit.

In short, Christmas socks offer a fantastic knitting opportunity, where love, imagination, and heart count as much as skill, because a stocking is always intended for someone special who is likely to treasure it forever. For this book, Interweave Press invited eighteen of today's most talented knitwear designers to create a Christmas stocking design that would offer knitting satisfaction and fun.

The inspired results range from classic to contemporary, from easy and bright to challenging and subtly complex in color or pattern. Tara Jon Manning's "Big Easy" can be knit in just a few hours on size 15 needles, while Candace Eisner Strick's stunning Austrian traveling-stitch design or Donna Kay's intricately patterned Scandinavian stocking require precision and concentration. Yet each of these, and every stocking in between, is beautiful, spirited, inventive, and unique.

We hope you'll love knitting, hanging, and filling these special stockings. May your holidays be merry and bright, and filled with creativity and joy.

HOW TO USE THIS BOOK

For each pattern, we've specified a generic yarn weight (such as worsted, heavy worsted, or bulky weight), with generous yardage approximations. This allows knitters to easily substitute yarns of choice. To replicate the look of the stocking as photographed, see the list of yarns used by the designers in the back of the book. We've also included a list of suppliers for these yarns; most companies will direct knitters to local yarn shops or websites that sell their yarns.

The designs are grouped by degree of difficulty, starting with easy patterns suitable for beginning knitters and progressing to more challenging projects.

Most of these socks are knit using basic sock-knitting techniques: Beginning at the top and knitting in the round, the leg of the sock is knit first; stitches are then divided into heel stitches and instep stitches; a heel flap is knit back and forth and "turned" with short rows, then stitches are picked up around the heel and instep and knitting in the round commences again. The gussets, or sides of the foot, are shaped with decrease rounds, the foot is knit, and the toe is shaped, again with decrease rounds.

The process isn't difficult; experiencing it just once de-mystifies the details (even the heel turning). First-time sock knitters may want to try our Miniature Stocking Ornament before beginning a full-size stocking.

A few of these projects, on the other hand, begin on straight nee-

The Parts of a Sock

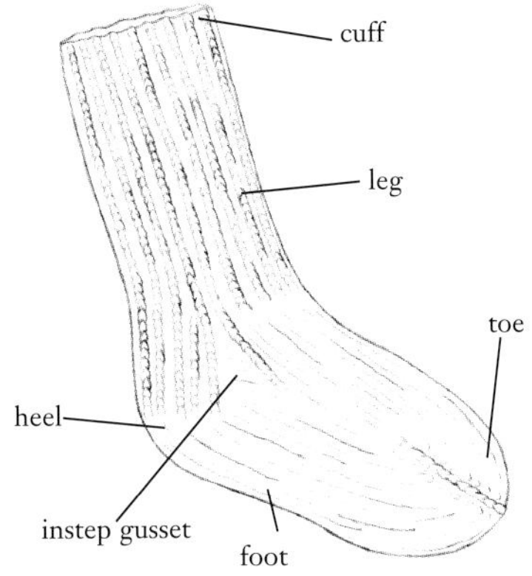

dles and include a seam. See specific pattern instructions for techniques used for each sock. A full list of abbreviations used and an illustrated glossary of basic techniques begins below.

For those with a Christmas stocking vision all their own, we also provide a set of basic stocking patterns for sport/double knitting weight, worsted weight, and bulky weight yarn that offer a few different techniques for heel and toe shaping. Use these patterns as a foundation to create your own Christmas stocking designs, adding embellishment, embroidery, and patterning as you wish. There's also an easy alphabet chart to add a name, date, or message to your design or to many of the stockings in this book.

ABBREVIATIONS AND GLOSSARY OF KNITTING TECHNIQUES

Knitting Gauge

To check gauge, cast on 30 to 40 stitches using recommended needle size. Work in pattern stitch until piece measures at least 4" (10 cm) from cast-on edge. Remove swatch from needles or bind off loosely, and lay swatch on flat surface. Place a ruler over swatch and count number of stitches across and number of rows down (including fractions of stitches and rows) in 4" (10 cm). Repeat two or three times on different areas of swatch to confirm measurements. If you have more stitches and rows than called for in instructions, use larger needles; if you have fewer, use smaller needles. Repeat until gauge is correct.

Reading Charts

Unless otherwise indicated, read charts from the bottom up. On right-side rows, read charts from right to left. On wrong-side rows, read charts from left to right. When knitting in the round, read charts from right to left for all rows.

Picking Up Heel Stitches

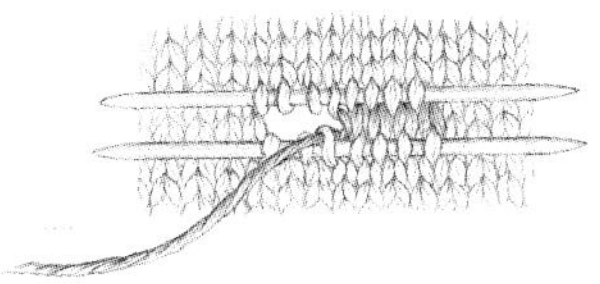

To begin heel, insert needles through stitches on either side of the contrasting waste yarn, then remove waste yarn.

Using Double-Pointed Needles

Begin by casting on stitches onto one double-pointed needle. Then divide the stitches evenly onto three needles. To join, lay the three needles in a triangle on a flat surface. Avoid twisted stitches by arranging the cast-on edge so that the bottom edge of each stitch faces the center of the triangle. Keeping the needles in this arrangement, pick them up, and use the fourth needle to begin knitting by inserting it into the first cast-on stitch and knitting with the working yarn that comes out of the last cast-on stitch. Because the needles have points at both ends, you can work around and around on them, just as you would with circular needles.

Arrange the needles in a triangle with the bottom edge of each stitch facing inward.

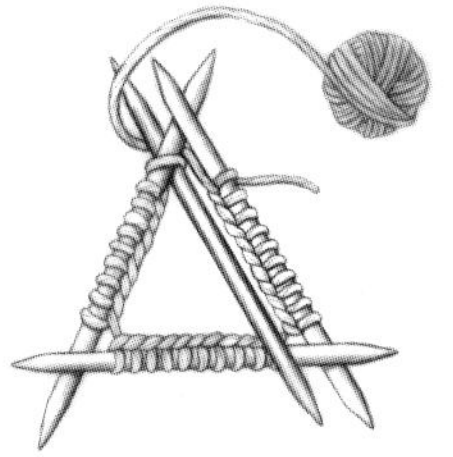

Use a fourth needle to knit the first cast-on stitch.

Invisible Seam

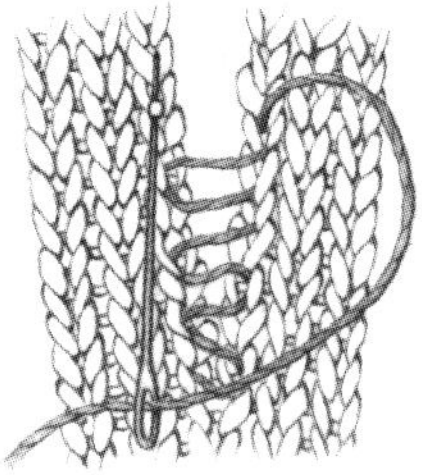

Working from the right side of the garment, place the pieces to be seamed on a flat surface, right sides up. Begin at the lower edge and work upward, row by row. Insert a threaded tapestry needle under two horizontal bars between the first and second stitches in from the edge on one side of the seam, and then under two corresponding bars on the opposite side. Continue alternating from side to side, pulling the yarn in the direction of the seam, not outward toward your body, to prevent the bars from stretching to the front. When the seam is complete, weave the tail end down through the seam allowance for two inches (5 cm).

Picking Up Gusset Stitches

The gussets are worked from stitches picked up along the two sides of the heel flap, after the heel has been turned. These stitches need to be picked up with right sides facing you. To pick up the stitches to join the heel with the instep, first work down the right side of the heel flap to pick up the needed stitches. Then work across the instep stitches and up the left side of the heel flap. (Right and left refer to the sides of the heel flap when the sock is right-side up, as though it is on your foot.)

Knitting Abbreviations

beg	beginning; begin; begins
bet	between
BO	bind off
CC	contrasting color
CD	central decrease—slip 2 st tog knitwise, k1, pass slipped stitches over the k stitch
cm	centimeter(s)
cn	cable needle
CO	cast on
cont	continue
dec(s)	decrease(s); decreasing
dpn	double-pointed needle(s)
foll	following
fwd	forward
g	gram(s)
inc	increase(s); increasing
k	knit
k1f&b	knit into front and back of same stitch
ktbl	knit through back loop
k2tog	knit two stitches together
kwise	knitwise
m	marker(s)
M1	make one stitch by lifting the horizontal running thread between two stitches and knitting into the back of it
M1-left slant	Make one, left slant. With left needle tip, pick up running strand between two stitches from front to back, knit strand through the back loop to twist.
M1-right slant	Make one, right slant. With left needle tip, pick up running strand between two stitches from back to front, knit strand through the front loop to twist.
MC	main color
mm	millimeter(s)
p	purl
p1f&b	purl into front and back of same stitch
ptbl	purl through back loop
patt(s)	pattern(s)
pm	place marker
psso	pass slipped stitch over
p2tog	purl two stitches together
pwise	purlwise
rem	remaining
rep	repeat
rev St st	reverse stockinette stitch
rib	ribbing
rnd(s)	round(s)
RS	right side
rsc	reverse single crochet
sc	single crochet
sk	skip
sl	slip
sl st	slip stitch (purlwise unless otherwise indicated)
ssk	slip 1 knitwise, slip 1 knitwise, k2 sl sts tog tbl
ssp	slip 1 kwise, slip 1 kwise, p2 sl sts tog tbl
st(s)	stitch(es)
St st	stockinette stitch
tbl	through the back loop
tog	together
WS	wrong side
wyb	with yarn in back
wyf	with yarn in front
yo	yarn over
*	repeat starting point (i.e. repeat from *)
* *	repeat all instructions between asterisks
( )	alternate measurements and/or instructions
[ ]	instructions that are to be worked as a group a specified number of times

Stranding Methods

Knit rows
Use your left hand to keep the pattern color below the tip of the left needle while your right forefinger brings the background color around the tip of the right needle to knit the stitch. Repeat this until the colors change.

Use your left forefinger to bring the pattern yarn around the needle and use the tip of the needle to draw the new stitch through while your right hand keeps the background color away from the needle tip and above the other stitches.

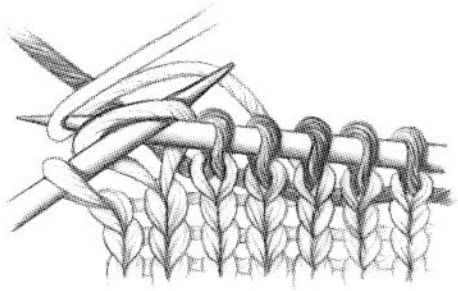

Right hand knits with background color, left hand carries pattern color.

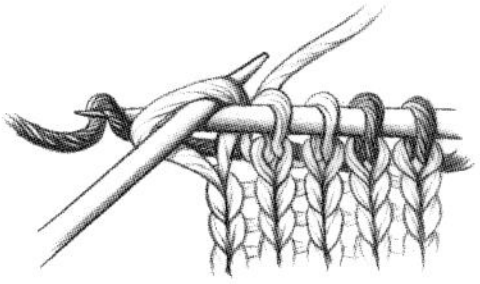

Right finger keeps background color above pattern color.

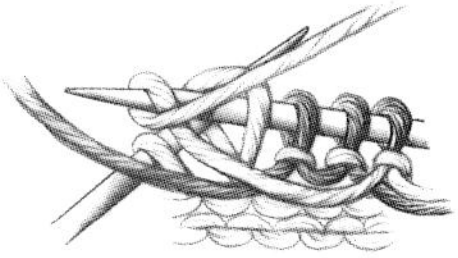

Left hand holds pattern color under stitch being purled.

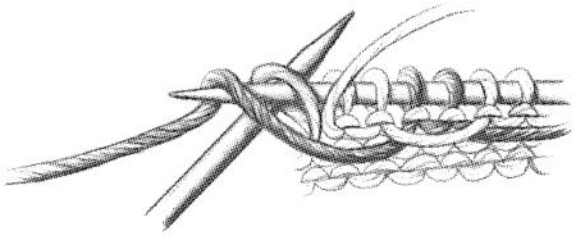

Right hand holds background color away from needle tips.

Purl rows
The purl row, although a little more difficult to learn, is worked the same way. Use your left hand to keep the pattern yarn below the purled stitches when it is not being worked.

Use your right hand to hold the background yarn up and away from the needle tips while your left forefinger passes the pattern yarn around the needle tip.

Provisional Cast-On

Place a loose slipknot of working yarn on needle. Hold waste yarn next to slipknot and wind working yarn under waste yarn, over needle, and in front of and then behind waste yarn for desired number of stitches. When you're ready to work in the opposite direction, remove waste yarn and pick up loops.

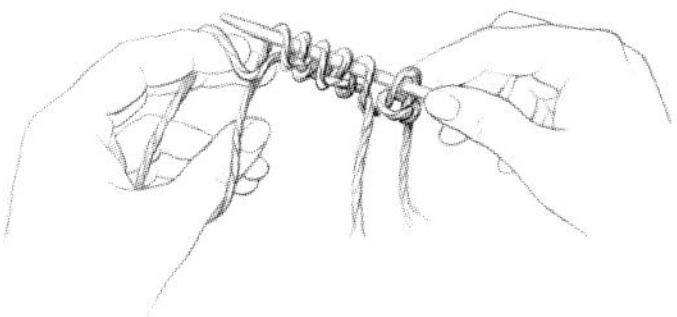

Intarsia

Use this method to work small areas of different colors without forming holes. These areas can be worked with small balls of the color wound onto bobbins and twisted over the adjacent color at every color join. Small areas can be worked with a loose length of yarn.

Work to the color change, then bring the color that has been used over the new color, and bring the new color up so that the yarns link or are twisted at the joining point.

Where irregular shapes are worked in the same design, you may need to carry some colors without working them for a number of stitches by weaving them in along the back. Look ahead one or two rows of the intarsia chart to decide where to position the yarn in preparation for the next row.

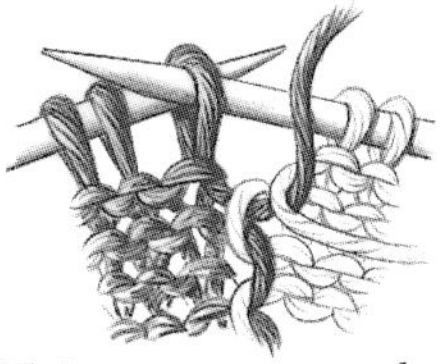

Twist one yarn over the other on the wrong side.

Continental (Long-Tail) Cast-On

Make a slipknot and place on right-hand needle, leaving a long tail. Place thumb and index finger of left hand between the two threads. Secure long ends with your other three fingers. Hold your hand palm up and spread thumb and index finger apart to make a V of yarn around them. There are four strands of yarn, 1, 2, 3, and 4 (Figure 1). Place needle under strand 1, from front to back. Place needle over top of strand 3 (Figure 2) and bring needle down through loop around thumb (Figure 3). Drop loop off thumb and, placing thumb back in the V configuration, tighten up resulting stitch on needle.

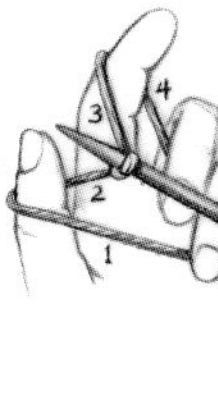

Figure 1

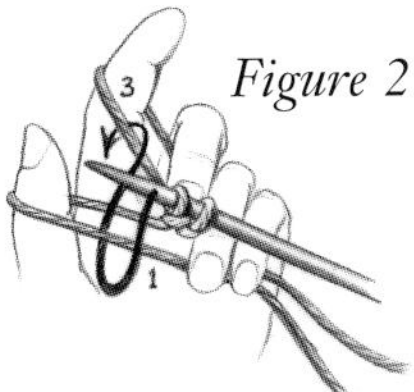

Figure 2

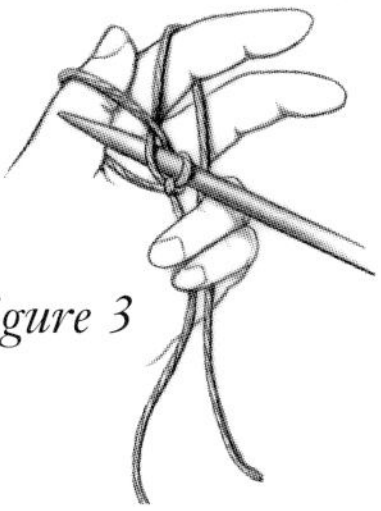

Figure 3

Short Row: Wrapping a Stitch

Figure 1

Figure 2

Work to turn point, slip next stitch purlwise to right needle. Bring yarn to front (Figure 1). Slip same stitch back to left needle (Figure 2). Turn work and bring yarn in position for next stitch, wrapping the stitch as you do so. **Note** Hide wraps in a knit stitch when right side of piece is worked in a knit stitch. Leave wrap if the purl stitch shows on right side. Hide wraps as follows: Knit stitch: On right side, work to just before wrapped stitch. Insert right needle from front, under the wrap from bottom up, and then into wrapped stitch as usual. Knit them together, making sure new stitch comes out under wrap. Purl stitch: On wrong side, work to just before wrapped stitch. Insert right needle from back, under wrap from bottom up, and put on left needle. Purl them together.

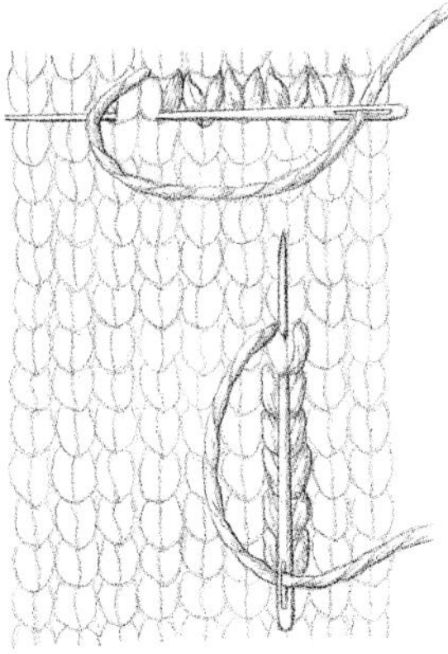

Duplicate Stitch

Horizontal: Bring threaded needle out from back to front at the base of the V of the knitted stitch you want to cover. *Working right to left, pass needle in and out under the stitch in the row above it and back into the base of the same stitch. Bring needle back out at the base of the V of the next stitch to the left. Repeat from *.

Vertical: Beginning at lowest point, work as for horizontal duplicate stitch, ending by bringing the needle back out at the base of the stitch directly above the stitch just worked.

I-Cord

With dpn, CO desired number of sts. *Without turning the needle, slide sts to other end of needle, pull yarn around back, and knit the sts as usual; rep from * for desired length.

Ssk Decrease

Slip two stitches knitwise one at a time (Figure 1). Insert point of left needle into front of two slipped stitches and knit them together through back loops with right needle (Figure 2).

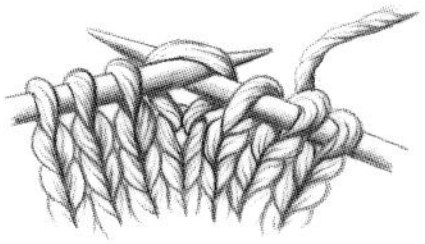

Figure 1

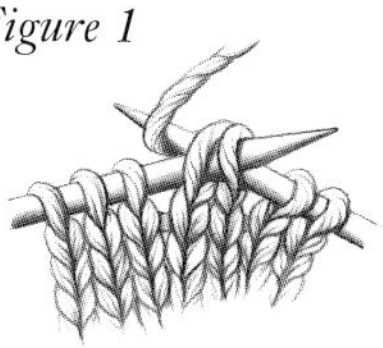

Figure 2

Crochet Chain Cast-On

Make a crochet chain 4 stitches longer than the number of stitches you need to cast on. Pick up and knit stitches through back loops of the crochet chain. Pull out the crochet chain to expose live stitches when you're ready to knit in the opposite direction.

Applied I-Cord

As I-cord is knitted attach it to the garment as follows: With garment RS facing and using a separate ball of yarn and circular needle, pick up the desired number of stitches along the garment edge. Slide these stitches down the needle so that the first picked-up stitch is near the opposite needle point. With double-pointed needle, cast on desired number of I-cord stitches. Knit across the I-cord to the last stitch, then knit the last stitch together with the first picked-up stitch on the garment, and pull the yarn behind the cord (pull the yarn in front of the cord for reverse I-cord). Knit to the last I-cord stitch, then knit the last I-cord stitch together with the next picked-up stitch. Continue in this manner until all picked-up stitches have been used.

Note When working attached I-cord, do not pick up every stitch. Work the edging for about 2" (5 cm), then lay the piece flat to make sure that the cord lies flat along the edge—if not pull out the necessary stitches and rework, picking up more or fewer stitches along the garment edge, as needed.

Three-Needle Bind-Off

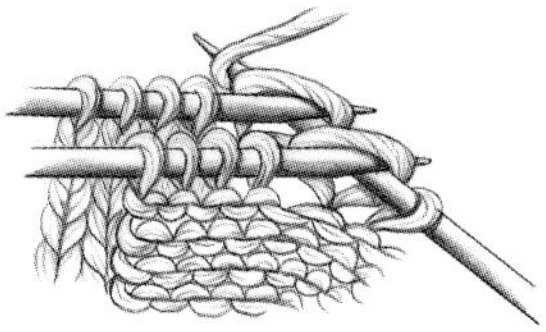

Place stitches to be joined onto two separate needles. Hold them with right sides of knitting facing together. *Insert a third needle into first stitch on each of the other two needles and knit them together as one stitch. Knit next stitch on each needle the same way. Pass first stitch over second stitch. Repeat from * until one stitch remains on third needle. Cut yarn and pull tail through last stitch.

Make 1 Knitwise Increase

Unless otherwise specified, use M1L. Make 1 left (M1L): With left needle tip, lift the strand between last knitted stitch and first stitch on left needle, from front to back (Figure 1). Knit the lifted loop throught back (Figure 2). Makes a left slant. Make 1 right (M1R): With left needle tip, lift the strand between last knitted stitch and first stitch on left needle, from back to front (Figure 3). Knit lifted loop through the front (Figure 4). Makes a right slant.

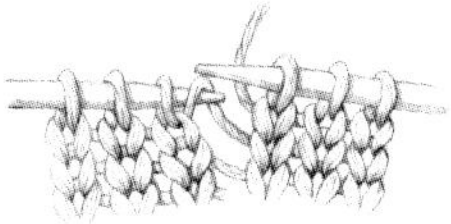

Figure 1

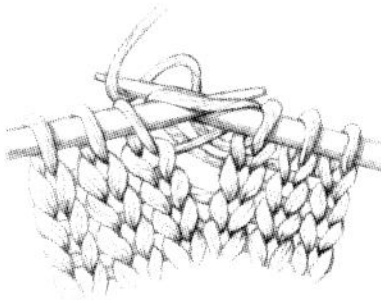

Figure 2

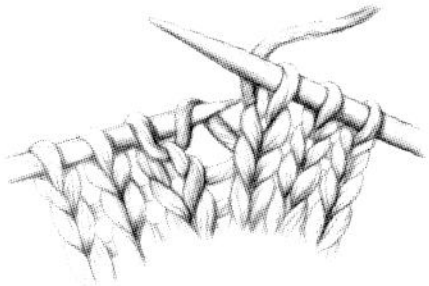

Figure 3

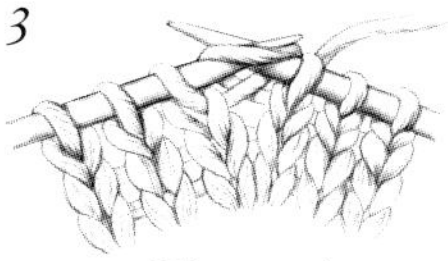

Figure 4

Kitchener Stitch

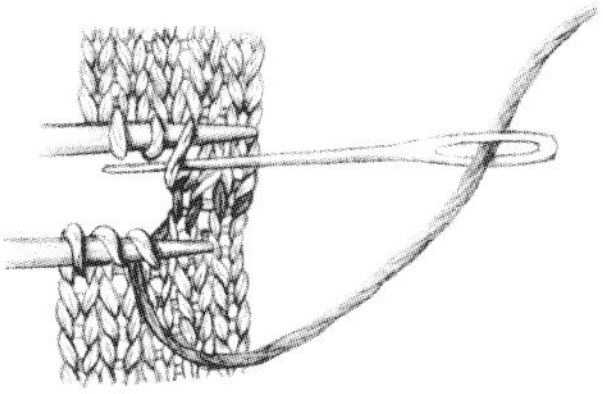

Step 1: Bring threaded needle through front stitch as if to purl and leave stitch on needle.

Step 2: Bring threaded needle through back stitch as if to knit and leave stitch on needle.

Step 3: Bring threaded needle through the same front stitch as if to knit and slip this stitch off needle. Bring threaded needle through next front stitch as if to purl and leave stitch on needle.

Step 4: Bring threaded needle through first back stitch as if to purl (as illustrated), slip that stitch off, bring needle through next back stitch as if to knit, leave this stitch on needle.

Repeat Steps 3 and 4 until no stitches remain on needles.

French Knot

Bring needle out of the knitted background from back to front, wrap yarn around needle one to three times, and use your thumb to hold it in place as you pull needle through the wraps into the background a short distance from where the thread first emerged.

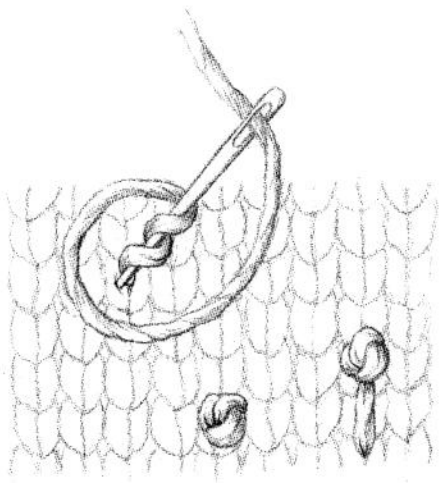

Chain (ch)

Make a slipknot on the hook. Yarn over the hook and draw it through the loop of the slipknot. Repeat, drawing the yarn through the last loop formed.

Single Crochet (sc)

Insert the hook into a stitch, yarn over the hook and draw a loop through the stitch, yarn over the hook (figure 1) and draw it through both loops on the hook (figure 2).

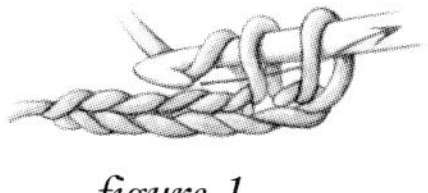

figure 1

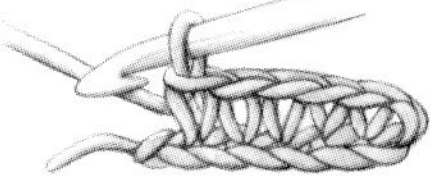

figure 2

SNOWY NIGHT GANSEY STOCKING

Lisa Carnahan

TRADITIONAL PURL STITCH MOTIFS CREATE A STARRY WINTER SCENE ON THIS GANSEY-STYLE STOCKING. WORKED IN THE ROUND, THE STOCKING USES THE TECHNIQUES OF BASIC SOCK CONSTRUCTION. THIS EASY-TO-KNIT STOCKING LOOKS BEST WHEN WORKED IN A SMOOTH, SOLID-COLORED YARN TO ACCENTUATE THE STITCHES.

Finished Size
About 7" (17.5 cm) across top of stocking; about 14" (35.5 cm) from top to heel; about 11" (28 cm) from heel to toe.

Yarn
Worsted weight yarn, approximately 275 yds (252 m) sage green.

Needles
Size 7 (4.5 mm): double-pointed needles (dpn). Adjust needle size if necessary to obtain the correct gauge.

Notions
Marker (m); tapestry needle.

Gauge
20 sts and 28 rows = 4" (10 cm) in St st.

STITCHES

Broken Rib:
Rnd 1: *K1, p1; rep from *.

Rnd 2: Knit.

Rep rnds 1-2 for pattern.

Garter Ridge Pattern:
Rnds 1 and 2: Knit.

Rnd 3: Purl.

Rnds 4 and 5: Knit.

LEG

CO 72 sts. Divide sts evenly on 3 needles. Place m and join being careful not to twist sts. Work 10 rnds of Broken Rib patt. Follow chart.

HEEL

Set-up row for heel flap: K18, slip rem 6 sts to next needle (this needle will hold the instep sts), turn. Next row: With empty needle, p18 and then p18 from the next needle; slip rem 6 sts to instep needle—36 sts on each of 2 needles.

Heel flap: (36 sts worked back and forth in rows)

Slip edge stitches purlwise.

Row 1: Sl 1, knit to end of row, turn.

Row 2: Sl 1, purl to end of row, turn.

Repeat these two rows until a total of 20 rows have been worked, ending with Row 2.

Turn heel:

Row 1: K21, ssk, k1, turn.

Row 2: Sl 1, p7, p2tog, p1, turn.

Row 3: Sl 1, k8, ssk, k1, turn.

Row 4: Sl 1, p9, p2tog, p1, turn.

Row 5: Sl 1, k10, ssk, k1, turn.

Row 6: Sl 1, p11, p2tog, p1, turn.

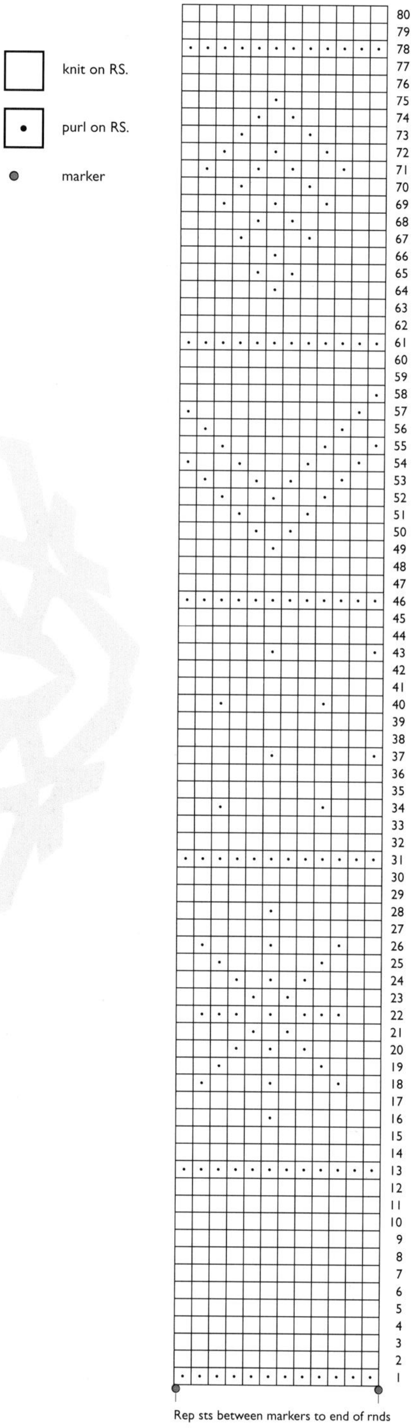

Row 7: Sl 1, k12, ssk, k1, turn.

Row 8: Sl 1, p13, p2tog, p1, turn.

Row 9: Sl 1, k14, ssk, k1, turn.

Row 10: Sl 1, p15, p2tog, p1, turn.

Row 11: Sl 1, k16, ssk, k1, turn.

Row 12: Sl 1, p17, p2tog, p1, turn.

Row 13: Sl 1, k18, ssk, k1, turn.

Row 14: Sl 1, p19, p2tog, p1, turn (22 sts rem).

Foot

Gusset: Pick up stitches for heel gusset as follows: Knit 11 sts. Using a free needle, knit next 11 sts. With this same needle, pick up 12 sts along edge of heel flap. With another free needle, knit 36 instep sts. With another free needle, pick up 12 sts along edge of heel flap and knit rem 11 sts. Row now ends at center of heel sts—23 sts on first needle, 36 sts on second needle, and 23 sts on third needle.

Rnd 1: Knit.

Rnd 2: Knit to last 3 sts of first needle, k2tog, k1; knit 36 instep sts on second needle; on third needle, k1, ssk, knit to end of needle.

Rep rnds 1 and 2 until 72 sts remain. Work even in St st until foot measures 9" (23 cm).

Toe shaping:

Rnd 1: Knit.

Rnd 2: Knit to last 3 sts of first needle, k2tog, k1; on second needle, k1, ssk, knit to last 3 sts of needle, k2tog, k1; on third needle, k1, ssk, knit to end of needle.

Rep rnds 1 and 2 until 28 sts rem. Knit across 7 sts from first needle onto the last needle. Instep needle now has 14 sts, with 14 sole sts on second needle.

Finishing

Using Kitchener stitch (see Glossary, page 9), graft remaining sts together. ***I-Cord loop:*** CO 4 sts and knit I-cord (see Glossary, page 8) for about 7" (18 cm) or desired length. Cut yarn and draw tail through rem sts. Stitch securely to top of stocking. If desired, use duplicate st and alphabet chart (on page 94) to embroider name into top panel of stocking.

Lisa Carnahan learned to knit as a child, but began knitting obsessively about 15 years ago. She has twice won awards in TKGA's National Design Competition, and her designs have appeared in Cast On *and* Knitters *and in the collections of Classic Elite, Fiber Trends, Berroco, and local yarn shops. Lisa is a Craft Yarn Council certified instructor and has taught beginners through advanced knitters. She's also a full-time wife and mother of three teenagers.*

CHRISTMAS RAINBOW SURPRISE

Barbara Albright

The intense colors of variegated wool yarn, blended by felting, make this stocking as unusual as it is easy and fast to knit. "As you knit, the colors change," says designer Barbara Albright, "and it feels like you're getting a surprise every step of the way." The felting process adds to the magic. "This sock literally flew off my needles because I couldn't wait to see how it felted," Barbara says.

Finished Size
Unfelted: Width 7" (18 cm); leg length 19" (48.5 cm); foot length 12" (30.5 cm). Felted: Width 6½" (16.5 cm); leg length 12½" (32 cm); foot 9½" (24 cm).

Yarn
Worsted weight yarn, approximately 265 yd (243 m). Do not use superwash wool or synthetics for felting projects.

Needles
Size 8 (5.0 mm): double-pointed needles (dpn). Size 8 (5.0 mm) 16" (40.5 cm) cir needle. Adjust needle size if necessary to obtain the correct gauge.

Notions
Markers (m); tapestry needle.

Gauge
18 sts and 28 rows = 4" (10 cm) in St st. (Because this stocking is felted, gauge is not critical.)

Note A cir needle may be used to make sock, changing to dpn when necessary.

Leg

CO 64 sts. Place m and join, being careful not to twist sts. Work St st for 4 rows.

Rnd 5: *K2tog, yo* rep around—64 sts.

Continue in St st until piece measures 14½" (37 cm).

Heel

Heel flap: (worked back and forth in rows)

Remove m and knit first 32 sts. Slip rem stitches onto spare needle and hold for instep. Slip edge stitches purlwise.

Row 1: (WS) Sl 1, purl to end.

Row 2: Sl 1, knit to end.

Work as above for 24 rows.

Turn heel:

Row 1: (WS) Sl 1, p20, p2tog, p1, turn.

Row 2: Sl 1, k11, ssk, k1, turn.

Row 3: Sl 1, p12, p2tog, p1, turn.

Row 4: Sl 1, k13, ssk, k1, turn.

Row 5: Sl 1, p14, p2tog, p1, turn.

MONDA
星期

Row 6: Sl 1, k15, ssk, k1, turn.

Row 7: Sl 1, p16, p2tog, p1, turn.

Row 8: Sl 1, k17, ssk, k1, turn.

Row 9: Sl 1, p18, p2tog, p1, turn.

Row 10: Sl 1, k19, ssk, k1 (22 sts rem).

Gusset: (RS) Pick up and k13 sts along side of heel flap, pm, knit across 32 instep sts, pm, pick up and k13 sts along other side of heel flap, k11 sts, pm (use a different color marker to denote beg of rnd) k11 sts—80 sts.

Rnd 1: Knit to within 3 sts of m, k2tog, k1; knit across 32 instep stitches to next marker, k1, ssk. Knit to end of rnd.

Rnd 2: Knit.

Rep these two rnds until 64 sts rem.

Foot

Work even in St st for 24 rnds. ***Toe shaping:*** Place 32 instep sts on first dpn, 16 sts of sole on second dpn and rem 16 sts on third dpn.

Rnd 1: Work even.

Rnd 2 (dec rnd): On first needle, k1, ssk, knit to last 3 sts, k2tog, k1. Needle #2: k1, ssk, knit to end. Needle #3: knit to last 3 sts, k2tog, k1.

Work above two rnds 5 times (10 rnds total). Rep rnd 2 until a total of 12 sts rem. Cut yarn and thread tail through remaining sts. Pull tight, secure, and fasten off. Weave in loose ends.

Finishing

Braided I-Cord hanger: With dpn, CO 4 sts. Starting each I-cord (see Glossary, page 8) with a different color section, work 3 pieces until each one is about 10" (25.5 cm) long. Braid the strips together, stretch braid lengthwise slightly when finished, then fold in half and attach securely to the back of the stocking. Folded hanger will be about 4" (10 cm) in height after felting. ***Felt the stocking:*** Felting is fun and almost magical. Place the knitted sock in a pillowcase or lingerie bag and close the top. Set the washer for the heavy-duty cycle, low water level, and hot water. If your water isn't especially hot, add a teakettle's worth of boiling water to the water in the washing machine. Place bag with sock inside into the washing machine, add a little liquid laundry or dishwashing detergent and let it agitate for about 10 minutes. Open the bag and take a look at the stocking. If it needs more felting, close bag and put it back in the washing machine for about 5 more minutes, resetting the cycle if needed. Check it again and continue until the sock looks felted. Rinse well, set machine to spin and remove excess moisture. Smooth out sock onto padded surface or folded towel, pat into shape and allow to dry.

Nebraska native Barbara Albright is the former editor of Chocolatier *magazine and a prolific journalist and cookbook author. Barbara's newest books include* Knitter's Stash *(Interweave Press, 2001),* Margaritas *(Andrews & McMeel, 2001) and* Rum *(Andrews & McMeel, 2001).*

SOCK MONKEY STOCKING

Linda Ligon

This easy-to-knit stocking with a vintage look is utterly disarming and simply wonderful. Linda Ligon's most recent Christmas stocking creation was inspired by the classic toy monkey made from socks. When you've completed the stocking, see the Supplier Guide (page 96) for information on ordering socks and instructions to make the monkey itself.

Finished Size
Approximately 7½" (19 cm) across top of stocking; 16½" (42 cm) from cuff to heel; 14½" (37 cm) from heel to toe.

Yarn
Worsted weight yarn, approximately 194 yds (178 m) ragg gray (MC); 50 yd (46 m) red (CC #1); 20 yd (19 m) winter white (CC #2).

Needles
Size 6 (4.mm): 16" (40.5 cm) cir needle and set of 5 double-pointed (dpn). Adjust needle size if necessary to obtain the correct gauge.

Notions
Markers (m); tapestry needle; about 1 yd (39 cm) of smooth waste cotton yarn to mark heel placement.

Gauge
18 sts and 28 rows = 4" (10 cm) in St st.

Leg

With CC #1 (red) yarn, CO 68 sts. Place m and join, being careful not to twist sts. Slipping m each rnd, work in k3, p1 rib for 24 rnds. Join CC #2 (white) and follow chart A, rnds 1–5, dec 2 sts on first rnd of chart—66 sts. Join MC (gray) as indicated on chart. After completing chart, and working only in MC, inc 2 sts on next rnd—68 sts. Work even in St st until leg measures about 13" (33 cm) from CO edge. ***Mark heel placement:*** On next rnd, k51, drop MC and join waste yarn, k17 to marker, then k17 past marker—34 sts worked in waste yarn. Drop waste yarn and slip the 34 waste yarn sts back onto left needle tip. Pick up MC where you left it and k34 waste yarn sts using MC. Cont rnds in St st and MC, sl m each rnd.

Foot

When foot measures about 7" (18 cm) from waste yarn sts, dec to 66 sts. Join CC #2 and work chart A again, this time reversing the colors. Work MC where CC #2 sts are shown on chart, and work in CC #2 where MC sts are shown. At the beg of last chart rnd, change to dpn and arrange sts as follows: Slip the first 16 sts after the marker onto needle #1, then sl 17 sts on needle #2, slip another 17 sts onto needle #3, and sl 16 sts onto needle #4—66 sts. Knit next rnd dec 2 sts as follows: k16 on needle #1. On needle #2, dec 1 st by working an ssk at beg of needle. On needle #3, knit across to the last 2 sts, k2tog (second dec made). On needle #4, k16—64 sts rem and each needle has 16 sts.

CC #2—winter white

MC — ragg gray

patt repeat

Chart A

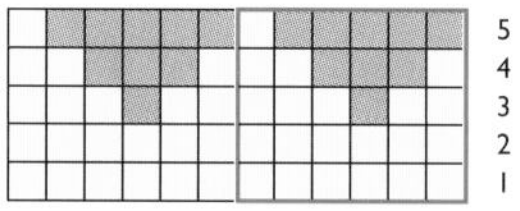

Leg: work rnds 1-5 as shown.
Toe area: Reverse colors in chart, working MC where CC #2 is shown, and CC #2 where MC is shown.

Toe shaping:

Rnd 1: Join CC #1, knit to last 2 sts of needle #1, k2tog. Work ssk at beg of needle #2, knit across to last 2 sts of needle #3, k2tog. Work ssk at beg of needle #4 then knit to marker, end of rnd.

Rnd 2: Knit.

Work these 2 rnds 7 times—36 rem. Now work rnd 1 only 6 times—12 sts rem. With needle #4, knit 3 sts from needle #1, slip 3 sts from needle 3 onto needle #2—you should now have 6 sole sts on one needle and 6 upper sts on one needle. Cut yarn leaving about 16" (41.5 cm) tail. Thread yarn tail onto tapestry needle and graft toe sts together with Kitchener stitch (see Glossary, page 9).

Heel

With back of stocking facing you, pm onto dp needle and then slip this needle though the 34 MC sts immediately below the waste yarn sts, then slip another dp needle through the 34 MC sts immediately above the waste yarn sts. Carefully remove waste yarn. Arrange sts so that the lower 34 sts are divided onto 2 dp needles, and the upper 34 sts are divided onto 2 needles—17 sts on each needle. Join CC #2 at marker and work 5 rnds, slipping marker each rnd.

Decrease rnd: On needle #1, work ssk immediately after marker, knit across to last 2 sts on next needle, k2tog. Work ssk on first 2 sts on needle #3, then knit across to last 2 sts on needle #4 and k2tog.

Join CC #1 and cont working dec rnd 12 more times—16 sts rem. Arrange sts so that the 8 sole sts are together on one needle, and the 8 upper sts are on another needle. Graft heel sts together with Kitchener st, same as toe instructions.

Finishing

I-Cord hanger: With dpn and CC #1, CO 4 sts. Knit 5" (13 cm) I-cord (see Glossary, page 8). BO all sts, cut yarn leaving about 18"(46 cm) yarn tail, and thread onto a tapestry needle. Pull needle and yarn through last st to secure, then fold I-cord in half and attach securely to the back of the stocking using yarn in tapestry needle. Weave in all ends.

Linda Ligon, founder of Interweave Press, has been knitting for half a century. This Christmas stocking, designed for her son-in-law, is ninth in an ever-growing collection of family holiday loot-wear.

THE CHUBBY SOCK

Lynn Gates

Beginning at the top with a corrugated rib, this short but sweet stocking is worked much like a regular sock—it just holds more goodies! Use the pattern charted here for the Fair Isle border, or substitute any Fair Isle pattern you wish.

Leg

With ecru and 16" (40 cm) circular needle, CO 80 sts. Place m and join, being careful not to twist stitches. Purl 2 rounds. Join medium green and work corrugated ribbing as follows:

Rnds 1–3: *K2 with ecru, p2 with medium green; rep from *.

Rnds 4–5: *K2 with ecru, p2 with dark green; rep from *.

Rnds 6–8: *K2 with ecru, p2 with medium green; rep from *.

With ecru only, purl 2 rnds.

With berry red only, k1 rnd, p1 rnd.

With medium green only, k1 rnd, p1 rnd.

With ecru, k1 rnd, decreasing 2 sts evenly—78 sts.

Fair Isle band: Work chart using berry red and dark green. When chart is complete, knit 1 round with ecru, increasing 2 sts evenly—80 sts.
With medium green, k1 rnd, p1 rnd, then proceed in St st. Keeping marker at center back, work decreases on either side of m as follows:
K 4 rnds, then decrease on next rnd: *k1, k2tog, k to 3 sts before m, ssk, k1. Knit 3 rnds.* Rep between * and * 3 times—72 sts. Knit around once more, stopping 17 sts before the marker.

Heel

Slip 17 sts before m and 17 sts after m onto empty dpn for heel—34 sts. Leave 38 rem sts on cir needle or place on holder for instep. ***Heel flap:*** (worked back and forth in rows) Join ecru and work in St st over 34 sts.

Row 1: Sl 1, knit across row.

Row 2: Sl 1, purl across row.

Repeat these two rows 6 more times—14 rows completed.

Turn heel:

Row 1: (RS) Sl 1, k18, ssk, k1, turn.

Row 2: Sl 1, p5, p2tog, p1, turn.

Finished Size
About 8" (20.5 cm) across top of stocking; 10½" (27 cm) from top to heel; 9" (23 cm) from heel to toe.

Yarn
Worsted weight yarn, approximately 120 yd (110 m) each ecru and medium green; 60 yd (55 m) each dark green and berry red.

Needles
Size 5 (3.75 mm): 16" (40 cm) circular and set of 5 double-pointed needles (dpn).

Gauge
19 sts and 25 rows = 4" (10 cm) in St st.

Notions
Marker (m); tapestry needle.

Row 3: Sl 1, k6, ssk, k1, turn.

Row 4: Sl 1, p7, p2tog, p1, turn.

Cont dec using one more stitch before dec until you have worked all sts, and ending on a WS (purl) row. 20 sts rem on heel. Break off ecru.

Foot

Gusset: Pick up circular needle with the instep sts, join medium green and pick up 8 sts along right side of heel flap, k first 10 sts off dpn, pm, knit next 10 sts and pick up 8 sts on other side of heel flap, work across 38 instep sts and work back to marker—74 sts. Work in rnds as follows:

Rnd 1: K15, k2tog, k40, ssk, k15.

Rnd 2: Knit.

Rnd 3: K14, k2tog, k40, ssk, k14.

Rnd 4: Knit.

Cont working dec every other row 5 times—64 sts rem. Continue in St st for 3" (7.5 cm), about 20 rows.

Toe shaping:

Rnd 1: Join ecru and knit all sts onto 4 dpn, beginning at m place 16 sts on each needle.

Rnd 2: On needle #1, k13, k2tog, k1. On needle #2, k1, ssk, k13. On needle #3, k13, k2tog, k1. On needle #4, k1, ssk, k13.

Rnd 3: Knit.

Repeat last two rnds 2 times, knitting 1 less st before and after each pair of decreases, then work rnd 2 every rnd until 4 sts rem on each needle.

Finishing

Graft end of toe together using Kitchener stitch (see Glossary, page 9) and weave in any loose ends. Make a hanging loop by picking up three sts with ecru at back of top border and working 4–5" (10–13 cm) of I-cord (see Glossary, page 8). Sew end of cord to top border, forming a loop. Steam lightly.

A yarn collector and avid knitter for more than 35 years, Lynn Gates learned her craft from a patient grandmother on a farm one summer. "I am really interested in shapings, sometimes subtle, that enhance the look and fit of a garment or piece with so little effort," she says. "It's also very rewarding to teach new knitters, and open up this whole other world for them." Lynn lives with her husband and two teenage boys in Colorado; the Chubby Sock is her first published design.

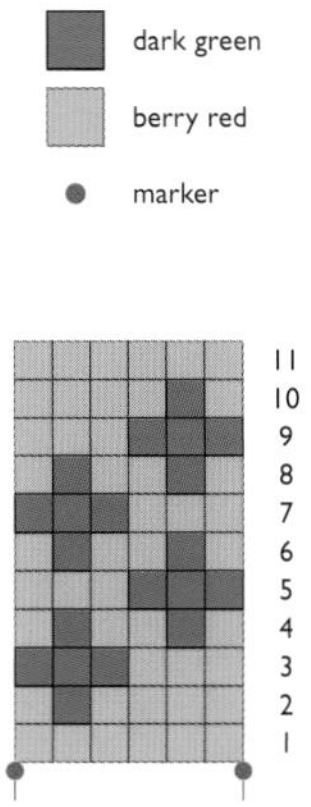

Rep patt between markers to end of rnd.

PAINTBOX POCKET STOCKING

Finished Size
About 6" (15 cm) across top of stocking; 15" (38 cm) from top to heel; 10" (26.5 cm) from heel to toe.

Yarn
Worsted weight yarn, approximately 300 yards (275 m) dark green (MC); small amounts of each of 4 other colors, blue, gold, fuschia, burnt orange for pockets; small amount of gray for the mouse.

Needles
Size 6 (4 mm): 16" (40 cm) circular (cir) and double-pointed needles (dpn). Adjust needle size if necessary to obtain the correct gauge.

Notions
Markers (m); tapestry needle; a small amount of fiberfill stuffing for the mouse; black embroidery floss for mouse eyes, nose, and whiskers; a few yards of smooth waste yarn for provisional CO.

Gauge
21 sts and 30 rounds = 4" (10 cm) in St st worked cir.

Barbara Albright

Inspired by the likes of Mondrian, this stocking is ideal for every modern artist. Knit the pockets in paintbox colors and add an artistic beret for the tiny mouse, which fits perfectly in the triangular pocket. Paintbrushes or any long objects fit in the long pocket, too.

Note Directions are given for the pockets we have photographed, but don't be afraid to make your own sizes of pockets. Make templates out of paper and position them on the stocking as you like them.

Leg

With cir needle, CO 64 sts using a provisional CO (see Glossary, page 7). Place m and join, being careful not to twist sts. Work in St st until piece measures 2½" (6.5 cm). Work turning rnd by purling 1 rnd on RS. Cont in St st until stocking measures 11¾" (30 cm) from turning rnd.

Heel

Heel flap: (work back and forth in rows) Remove m and knit first 32 sts. Slip rem 32 sts onto separate needle and hold for instep. Slip sts purlwise.

Row 1: (WS) Sl 1, p31.

Row 2: Sl 1, k31.

Work as above for 24 rows.

Turn heel:

Row 1: (WS) Sl 1, p20, p2tog, p1, turn.

Row 2: Sl 1, k11, ssk, k1, turn.

Row 3: Sl 1, p12, p2tog, p1, turn.

Row 4: Sl 1, k13, ssk, k1, turn.

Row 5: Sl 1, p14, p2tog, p1, turn.

Row 6: Sl 1, k15, ssk, k1, turn.

Row 7: Sl 1, p16, p2tog, p1, turn.

ARTISTS' SOFT
PASTEL

Row 8: Sl 1, k17, ssk, k1, turn.

Row 9: Sl 1, p18, p2tog, p1, turn.

Row 10: Sl 1, k19, ssk, k1.

22 sts rem and RS is facing.

Foot

Gusset: With cir needle, pick up and k13 sts along side of heel flap, pm, k32 held instep sts, pm, pick up and k13 sts along other side of heel flap, k11 sts of under heel, pm (use a different color marker to denote beg of rnd) k11 sts—80 sts. Join and work cir.

Rnd 1: Knit to within 3 sts of m, k2tog, k1; knit across 32 instep sts to next marker, k1, ssk. Knit to end of rnd.

Rnd 2: Knit one rnd.

Rep these two rnds until 64 sts rem. Work even in St st for 4" (10 cm). ***Toe shaping:*** Place 32 instep sts on first dpn, 16 sts of sole on second dpn and rem 16 sts on third dpn.

Rnd 1: Work even.

Rnd 2 (dec rnd): On needle #1, k1, ssk, knit to last 3 sts, k2tog, k1. On needle #2, k1, ssk, knit to end. On needle #3, knit to last 3 sts, k2tog, k1.

Work above 2 rnds 5 times for a total of 10 rnds—44 sts. Rep rnd 2 until a total of 12 sts rem. Cut yarn and thread tail on a tapestry needle, pull yarn through rem sts. Pull tight, secure, and fasten off. Weave in loose ends.

Long Rectangular Pocket

CO 9 sts. Work in St st, slipping first st in each row purlwise, until rectangle measures 9½" (24 cm) long. BO.

Top 2-Color Rectangular Pocket

CO 16 sts. Work in St st, slipping first st in each row purlwise, until square measures 1½" (3.8 cm) long. Change to a second color and knit ½" (1.3 cm) longer. BO.

Triangular Pocket

CO 1 st.

Row 1: (RS) K1f&b—2 sts.

Row 2: P2.

Row 3: K1, M1, k1—3 sts.

Row 4: P3.

Row 5: Sl 1, M1 right slant, k1, M1 left slant, k1—5 sts.

Row 6: P5.

Row 7: Sl 1, M1 right slant, k3, M1 left slant, k1—7 sts.

Row 8: P7.

Row 9: Sl 1, M1 right slant, k5, M1 left slant, k1—9 sts.

Row 10: P9.

Cont inc every other row until 21 sts are on needle. BO.

Bottom Solid Square Pocket

CO 18 sts. Work in St st, slipping first st in each row purlwise, until square measures 3½" (9 cm) long. BO.

Bottom 2-Color Pocket

CO 12 sts. Work in St st, slipping first st in each row purlwise, until square measures 2¼" (5.5 cm) long. Change to second color and knit ¾" (2 cm) longer. BO.

Mouse

CO 18 sts, leaving a yarn tail that will be used to create the mouse's tail. Place m and join, being careful not to twist sts. Work St st until piece measures 1½" (3.8 cm). ***Shape nose:*** Dec 3 sts evenly spaced around next rnd—15 sts rem. Knit 1 rnd. Rep these two rnds until 6 sts rem. K2tog around. Cut yarn and thread tail through rem 3 sts. Pull tight, secure, and fasten off. ***Finishing:*** Stuff mouse with stuffing. Thread some yarn through the end of the mouse and draw the end together to seal in stuffing. Add two pieces of yarn next to tail yarn by sewing a piece of yarn through the end of the mouse and pulling it halfway through rear end; braid the 3 strands together to achieve desired tail length. Tie a knot in the end of the braid and trim end of tail. With black embroidery floss, sew on whiskers, eyes and nose.

Mouse Beret

CO 4 sts, leaving a tail to create the cap's "stem." Knit in garter st (k every row) for 4" (10 cm). BO, leaving tail; thread tail through tapestry needle. Gather one long side (on stem side) of the strip by slipping the tapestry needle through the very edges of the projecting set of garter stitch loops and pull to gather. Sew the CO and BO sts to each other to create a circle. Add two pieces of yarn next to the stem yarn by sewing a piece of yarn through the center of the hat and pulling it halfway through the hat; braid the 3 strands together to achieve the desired stem length. Attach beret to mouse.

Finishing

Weave in loose ends. Block all pieces to measurements. With yarn threaded on a tapestry needle, turn top edge in and attach loose stitches of hem to the stocking. ***I-Cord hanger:*** With dpn, CO 4 sts. Work I-cord (see Glossary, page 8) until 6" (15 cm) long. Fold I-cord hanger in half and attach to stocking top. Attach pockets to stocking as desired.

Nebraska native Barbara Albright is the former editor of Chocolatier *magazine and a prolific journalist and cookbook author. Barbara's newest books include* Knitter's Stash *(Interweave Press, 2001),* Margaritas *(Andrews & McMeel, 2001) and* Rum *(Andrews & McMeel, 2001)*

THE BIG EASY

Tara Jon Manning

A fun, playful and QUICK stocking to knit for you and yours.

Finished size
About 7" (18 cm) across top of stocking; about 16¼" (41 cm) from top to heel; about 10½" (26.5 cm) from heel to toe.

Yarn
Super bulky-weight yarn, approximately 57 yds (52 m) each red, green, and natural.

Needles
Size 15 (10 mm): double-pointed needles (dpn). Adjust needle size if necessary to obtain the correct gauge.

Gauge
8 sts and 14 rows = 4" (10 cm) in St st.

Notions
Crochet hook (medium to large); markers (m); 2 stitch holders; tapestry needle.

Leg

With natural color and dpn, CO 32 sts. Place m and join, being careful not to twist stitches. Work St st (as shown here) or seed stitch cuff for 9 rnds or desired length. If working St st, purl one round at end of cuff. Follow chart for rnds 1–24 of patt.

Heel

Place next 8 sts on an empty needle, place next 16 sts on another empty needle, slip rem 8 sts onto end of needle #1. ***Heel flap:*** (worked back and forth in rows). Join green and work as follows:

Row 1: (RS) Sl 1, k15.

Row 2: Sl 1, p15.

Rep above 2 rows for 14 rows.

Turn heel:

Row 1: (RS) K10 sts, ssk, k1, turn.

Row 2: Sl 1, p5, p2tog, p1, turn.

Row 3: Sl 1, k6, ssk, k1, turn.

Row 4: Sl 1, p7, p2tog, p1, turn.

Row 5: Sl 1, k8, ssk, turn.

Row 6: Sl 1, p8, p2tog—10 sts rem.

Row 7: Join natural and k10.

Foot

Gusset: (RS) Using empty needle (#1) pick up 8 sts along side edge of heel flap, pm; k16 instep sts from needle #2, pm; with needle #3, pick up 8 sts along other side edge of heel flap then k5 sts from underheel, pm (use different color marker to indicate beg of rnd) and slip 5 rem underheel sts onto needle 1—42sts.

Rnd 1: Knit to within 3 sts of first m, k2tog, k1, knit across instep sts on needle #2, slip marker, work k1, ssk at beg of needle #3, k to end of rnd.

Rnd 2: Knit.

Rep rnds 1 and 2 until 32 sts rem, changing colors as needed. Cont working in St st stripes of 4 rnds each (natural, red, green, natural) until foot measures about 5" (12.5 cm). ***Shape toe***: Join red.

Rnd 1: On needle #1, k until 3 sts rem, k2 tog, k1. On needle #2, k1, ssk, k until 3 sts rem, k2tog, k1. On needle #3, k1, ssk, k to end.

Rnd 2: Knit.

Rep rnds 1 and 2 until 8 sts rem. Divide rem sts onto two dpns, knitting across where needed. Graft toe sts together using Kitchener stitch (see Glossary, page 9).

Finishing

Weave in all ends, block to shape. ***I-Cord hanger:*** With dpn and natural, CO 4 sts. Knit I-cord (see Glossary, page 8) until about 10" (25.5 cm) in length. Break off yarn leaving an 8" (20.5 cm) tail. Thread tail on tapestry needle, draw through sts and fasten off. Fold cord in half and attach securely to inside of stocking cuff.

Tara Jon Manning frequently contributes to Interweave Knits, *and owns Over the Moon Cafe & Mercantile, a knitting, gift, and espresso shop in Longmont, Colorado. Tara studied textile and apparel design and fiber arts at Colorado State University; her thesis, "Aran Hand Knitting, Design, History and Technique: A Contemporary Collection" combined in-depth historic research, design analysis, and a collection of six Aran-inspired hand-knit garments.*

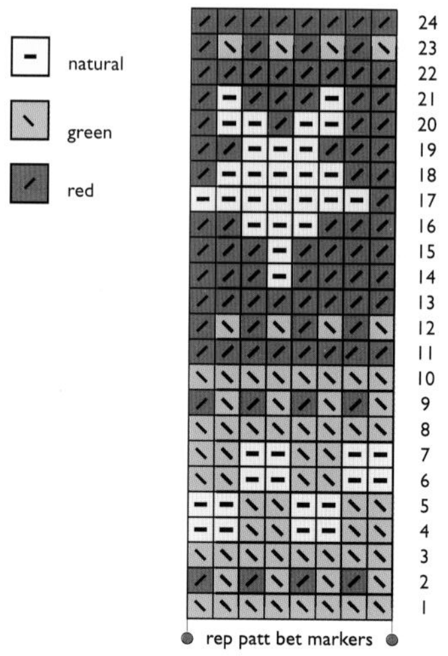

KEEPSAKE BABY STOCKING

Jennifer Carpenter

THIS SENTIMENTAL CHRISTMAS STOCKING IS PERFECT FOR A BABY'S FIRST CHRISTMAS, AND MAKES A SWEET MEMENTO OF BABY'S FIRST YEAR. "THE TWISTED CORD, ATTACHED TO THE CUFF FOR HANGING THE STOCKING, IS A FAVORITE EMBELLISHMENT OF MINE," SAYS DESIGNER JENNIFER CARPENTER. "IT'S USEFUL ANYWHERE A DECORATIVE CORD IS NEEDED."

Finished Size
About 5" (13cm) across top of stocking; 10" (25.5) top to heel; 6½" (16.5) heel to toe.

Yarn
Worsted weight chenille yarn, approximately 60 yd [55 m] each sky blue (color B) and teal (color D); worsted weight bouclé yarn, 100 yd [92 m] natural white (color C). Metallic yarn, 20 yd [19 m] gold (color A).

Needles
Size 7 (4.5mm): double pointed needles (dpn). Adjust needle size if necessary to obtain the correct gauge.

Notions
Wallet-size baby photo, clear acetate cut to same size as baby photo, ½" [1.4 cm] wide sheer blue ribbon, 2 large sequins, 2 small beads, 4 bells, ½" [1.4 cm] wide metallic ribbon, light blue sewing thread, sewing and tapestry needles.

Gauge
18 sts and 28 rows = 4" (10 cm) in St st.

STITCHES

Braid Pattern (Nancy Bush, *Folk Socks*, Interweave Press):

Rnd 1: * K1 with color A, k1 with color B; repeat from * around.

Rnd 2: Bring both colors to the front of the work. Keep them in the same order as on previous round. *P1A, p1B, always bringing the next color to be used OVER the top of the last color used. Repeat from * around.

Rnd 3: *P1A, p1B, always bringing the next color to be used UNDER last color used. Repeat from * around.

LEG

Braided edging: Make a slip knot with yarns A and B, CO 49 sts using the continental CO (see Glossary, page 7), with yarn A over the thumb and yarn B over the index finger during the CO process. Remove the loop formed by the slip knot after all sts have been cast on—48 sts. Arrange the sts on dpns so that there are 12 sts on each of 4 needles, place m at beg of rnd. Work 3 rounds in Braid Pattern. Break off yarns A and B, join yarn C and work in k2, p2 ribbing for 4" (10 cm). ***Leg:*** Rejoin yarn B, break off yarn C, and work 2 rnds St st. Join yarn D, and work 2 rnds St st. Cont stripe pattern as established, working 2 rnds with color B and 2 rnds with color D alternately for about 5½" (14 cm), working last two rnds in Color D.

Loosely strand color not in use up along each rnd beg to avoid breaking and starting new color every 2 rnds.

Heel

Divide for heel: Break off Color D and slip the 12 sts from needle #3 onto needle #4—24 sts, holding aside 12 sts each on the other two needles for instep. Join color C at the end of needle #4, and p24 sts on WS. Now work back and forth in Rev St st as folls:

Row 1: (RS) P24, turn.

Row 2: (WS) K24, turn.

Rep rows 1 and 2 until heel flap measures 2½" (6.5 cm), ending on a WS row.

Turn heel: cont in Rev St st.

Row 1: (RS) P14, p2tog, p1, turn.

Row 2: Sl 1 pwise, k5, ssk, k1, turn.

Row 3: Sl 1, p6, p2tog, p1, turn.

Row 4: Sl 1, k7, ssk, k1, turn.

Row 5: Sl 1, p8, p2tog, p1, turn.

Row 6: Sl 1, k9, ssk, k1, turn.

Row 7: Sl 1, p10, p2tog, p1, turn.

Row 8: Sl 1, k11, ssk, k1, turn.

Row 9: Sl 1, p12, p2tog, turn.

Row 10: (WS) Sl 1, k12, ssk, turn.

There are 14 sts remaining on needle. Break yarn.

Foot

Gusset: With RS facing, join yarn B, and pick up and knit 13 sts along right side of heel flap, knit across the 24 instep sts, pick up and knit 13 sts along left side of heel flap, knit across half of the heel sts (7), pm to indicate beg of rnds, and slip the other half of heel sts (7) onto needle #1—64 sts. Change to St st stripe pattern as before.

Rnd 1: Knit.

Rnd 2: Knit to last 3 sts of needle #1, k2tog, k1. Knit across the 24 instep sts on needles #2 and #3. At beg of needle #4, k1, ssk, knit to end of rnd.

Work rnds 1 and 2 a total of 8 times—48 sts rem. Work even on 48 sts until foot measures 3" (7.5 cm) from last row of heel worked in yarn C. Break yarns B and D. ***Shape toe:*** Rejoin yarn C, and knit 1 rnd. Change to Rev St st, and work 2 rnds. Begin decreasing for toe every rnd as folls:

Decrease Rnd: Purl to the last 3 sts of needle #1, p2tog, k1. On needle #2, k1, p2tog, purl to the end of needle. On needle #3, purl to the last 3 sts, p2tog, k1. On needle #4, k1, p2tog, p to end.

Work decrease rnd 9 times until 12 sts rem—3 sts on each needle. With needle #4, k3 sts from needle #1, then slip 3 sts from needle #3 onto needle #2. You should now have 6 upper sts on one needle and 6 sole sts on one needle. Graft toe sts together using Kitchener stitch (see Glossary, page 9). Weave in all loose ends.

Finishing

Attach photo: Cut a piece of clear acetate the same size as the photo you have chosen for decorating your stocking, approximately 2½" × 3" (6.5 × 7.5 cm). Place acetate over photo, and using a hole punch place holes in each corner. Thread sheer ribbon through a tapestry needle, and beginning with bottom right corner and moving counter-clockwise, sew photo onto stocking, tying ends of ribbon together on WS of stocking. Decorate the bottom corners with beads, bells, and sequins as shown. Using a 10" (25.5 cm) length of sheer and metallic ribbon held together, make a bow for top of photo. Trim ends, and sew bow to stocking with sewing thread, hiding the holes where photo is attached. If desired, use a fabric pen to write baby's name and date of birth on the ends of ribbon. ***Twisted cord:*** Cut 45" (144.5 cm) lengths of yarns A and B. Hold together, and tie one end to a door knob or chair rail, and attach the other end with a slip knot to a dpn. Holding the dpn in your hand so the yarns are not slack, twist them clockwise until they begin to kink. Fold the yarns in half, allowing the kink to travel all the way up so that they are evenly twisted. Tie a knot to secure them, weave in ends, and sew to cuff of stocking with a bead or button and sewing thread. ***Note:*** See page 96 for information on ordering a notions kit for this stocking.

Jennifer Carpenter is the co-owner of Sophie's Yarns in Philadelphia. She teaches knitting there and through Temple University's adult education project. Jennifer learned to knit from her grandmother during summer visits to her lakeside cabin in Northern Minnesota, and is happiest, she says, working on rustic warm "Minnesota" sweaters and traditional Fair-Isle mittens in natural luxury yarns.

GIANT JESTER STOCKING

Sandy Cushman

THIS JOYOUS AND WHIMSICAL SOCK USES BRIGHT COLORS, AN EASY STRIPE PATTERN, AND BELLS TO CELEBRATE THE FUN SIDE OF THE HOLIDAYS. THE TOP ZIG-ZAG "RUFFLE" IS KNITTED FLAT AND THEN THE WORK IS REVERSED, CREATING THE CUFF.

Finished Size
About 6½" (16.5 cm) across top of stocking; 17¼" (43.5 cm) from cuff to heel; 11½" (29 cm) heel to toe.

Yarn
Worsted weight yarn, approximately 160 yd (147 m) turquoise (color D); 160 yd (147 m) dark red (color C); 100 yd (92 m) bright green (color A); 100 yd (92 m) purple (color B).

Needles
Size 8 (5.0 mm): 24" (61 cm) circular. Size 7 (4.5 mm): set of 5 double-pointed needles (dpn). Adjust needle size if necessary to obtain the correct gauge.

Notions
Markers (m); tapestry needle; size 7 (4.5 mm) crochet hook. Optional: 2 or more small decorative bells to attach to stocking cuff.

Gauge
20 sts and 24 rows = 4" (10 cm) in St st.

Note This stocking has a definite back and front; the round begins and ends at the back. The garter stitch top is worked back and forth, then joined, and the body of the stocking is worked in the round. The heel is set in after the stocking is knit to the toe.

Leg

Cuff: With larger needle and color A, cast on 81 sts. Knit one row. Join color B and work next 2 rows as follows:

Row 1: *K1, yo, k2, sl 1-k2tog-psso, k2, yo; rep from * 10 times, end k1.

Row 2 and all even rows: Knit.

Alternating colors A and B, rep rows 1 and 2 five more times—12 rows.

Next row: With color B, work as follows: *K3, sl 1-k2tog-psso, k2; rep from * 10 times, end k1—61 sts.

Next row: With color B, knit rnd and dec 1 st—60 sts.

Next row: With color A, knit. At end of row, pm, change to dpn and join knitting being careful not to twist sts.

Place 15 sts on each needle. Purl 1 row with color A. Knit 2 rnds with color B. Cut colors A and B and attach colors C and D. Knit 2 rnds with color C; knit 2 rnds with color D; and knit 2 more rnds with color C. Reverse direction by turning stocking inside out.

Cont working in the round, alternating two knit rows of color C and two knit rows of color D until piece measures about 13.5" (34 cm) with cuff turned down. ***Insert waste yarn to mark heel:*** Work across needles #1 and #2 (30 sts) and drop main yarn. With waste yarn, knit across next 30 sts. Drop waste yarn. Pick up main yarn at beg of needle #3 and work to end of rnd. Cont alternating colors C and D as before, knitting 2 rnds of

each until piece measures about 2" (5 cm) from waste yarn.

Foot

Still alternating 2 rows each of color C and D, dec on 2nd row of each color as follows: On needle #1, k1, ssk, knit rem sts. On needle #2, knit to last 3 sts, k2tog, k1. On needle #3, k1, ssk, knit rem sts. On needle #4, work to last 3 sts, k2tog, k1. When piece measures about 5" (12.5 cm) from waste yarn, and still working decreases, cut colors C and D. Attach colors A and B and cont working in stripes and dec until 12 sts rem. Put sts on holder.

Heel

Pick up sts for heel by placing dpns through 30 sts on either side of waste yarn (see Glossary, page 5). Carefully remove waste yarn. Arrange sts so that each needle has 15 sts. With color A, M1 using the running strand between leg and foot sts, knit 30 sts from needles #1 and #2, pick up 2 sts using the running strand between needles #2 and #3, knit 30 sts from needles #3 and #4, pm, pick up 1 st—64 sts. ***Heel decreases:*** Cont alternating colors A and B, work dec rnds as follows:

Rnd 1: On needles #1 and 3, k1, ssk, knit rem sts. On needles #2 and #4, work to last 3 sts on needle, k2tog, k1.

Rnd 2: Knit.

Work last 2 rnds 20 times—24 sts rem. Work Rnd 1 rnd every rnd 3 times—12 sts. Work 1 rnd even. Place 12 rem sts on holder.

Finishing

Place 6 sts each onto 2 dpn for top and bottom of foot. Graft sts together using Kitchener stitch (see Glossary, page 9). Graft heel sts together in same manner. ***Top flap/ruffle:*** Weave cuff seam on RS carefully matching stripes. Turn cuff over on last green row. With crochet hook and dark red (color C) work picot as follows: Into every knit st, *2 single crochet in each of next two sts, work single crochet in next st, ch 3, single crochet into the knit st to form picot.* Rep from * to end of row. ***I-Cord hanger:*** With green (color A) CO 4 sts and knit I-cord (see Glossary, page 8) about 7" (18 cm) long. Cut yarn leaving about a 6" (15 cm) tail. With yarn threaded on a tapestry needle sew through all sts, pull gently to close. Imbed yarn tail through center of I-cord to secure. Fold I-cord in half and sew to inside of flap even with middle of heel. Steam lightly if desired. Sew bells to points of top ruffle if desired.

Sandy Cushman earned a BFA in painting at the Rhode Island School of Design, and supported her art with jobs from working on a lobster boat to designing textiles. She moved to Dolores, Colorado, in 1996 and, she says, "got serious about designing knitwear." A frequent contributor to Interweave Knits, *Sandy's passion is working with color.*

SNOWMAN AT MIDNIGHT

Nicky Epstein

NICKY EPSTEIN CREATED THIS EASY STOCKING WITH KIDS IN MIND. USING THE THREE-DIMENSIONAL EMBELLISHMENT TECHNIQUES NICKY IS KNOWN FOR, THE SNOWMAN AND SNOWFLAKES ARE KNIT SEPARATELY AND ATTACHED TO THE MID-NIGHT-BLUE SOCK. ADD YOUR FAVORITE SNOWMAN-BUILDER'S NAME IF YOU LIKE.

Finished Size

About 7"(18 cm) across top of stocking; 16½" (42 cm) from cuff to heel; 10½" (26.5 cm) from heel to toe.

Yarn

Heavy worsted weight, approximately 185 yd (170 m) dark blue; 100 yd (92 m) natural; 50 yd (46 m) berry, small amounts black and orange.

Needles

Size 7 (4.5 mm): straight needles. Size 6 (4 mm): straight and double-pointed needles (dpn).

Notions

Marker (m); stitch holders; tapestry needle.

Gauge

16 sts and 22 rows = 4" (10 cm) in St st.

LEG

Cuff: With larger size needles and blue, CO 61 sts. Work back and forth in St st (purl 1 row, knit 1 row) for 12 rows, end with a knit row. *Next row:* (WS) Knit across for turning ridge. Beg with a knit row, cont in St st for 9 rows more. ***Leg:*** Purl 1 row, knit 1 row. Work even in St st for 37 rows, end with a purl row.

Dec row: (RS) K1, ssk, knit to last 3 sts, k2tog, k1—59 sts.

Rep dec row every 10th row 3 times—53 sts. Work even until 81 rows above cuff, end with purl row.

HEEL

Divide for heel: From right side, sl first 13 sts to holder for right half of heel, sl next 27 sts to second holder for instep, sl rem 13 sts to free needle for left half of heel.

Left half of heel:

Row 1: P across.

Row 2: Sl 1, k 12.

Rep these 2 rows 8 times—18 rows on heel.

Turn heel:

Row 1: (WS) P2, p2tog, p1, turn.

Row 2: Sl 1, k3, turn.

Row 3: P3, p2tog, p1, turn.

Row 4: Sl 1, k4, turn.

Row 5: P4, p2tog, p1, turn.

Row 6: Sl 1, k5, turn.

Row 7: P5, p2tog, p1, turn.

Row 8: Sl 1, k6, turn.

Row 9: P6, p2tog, p1.

8 sts rem. Break yarn, sl sts to holder.

Right half of heel:

From wrong side, sl 13 sts of right half of heel to free needle.

Row 1: K across.

Row 2: Sl 1, p 12.

Rep these 2 rows 8 times—18 rows on heel.

***Turn heel*:**

Row 1: K2, ssk, k1, turn.

Row 2: Sl 1, p3, turn.

Row 3: K3, ssk, k1, turn.

Row 4: Sl 1, p4, turn.

Row 5: K4, ssk, k1, turn.

Row 6: Sl 1, p5, turn.

Row 7: K5, ssk, k1, turn.

Row 8: Sl 1, p6, turn.

Row 9: K6, ssk, k1.

8 sts rem. Break yarn.

Foot

From wrong side, sl these sts to free needle. From right side, knit across 8 sts of right half heel; with same needle, pick up and k9 sts along side edge of heel flap, k across 27 sts of instep, pick up and k9 sts along edge of left half heel flap, k8 sts of left heel from holder—61 sts. Purl 1 row.

Gusset:

Row 1: (RS) K14, k2tog, k29, ssk, k14—59 sts.

Row 2 and all WS rows: P.

Row 3: K13, k2tog, k29, ssk, k13.

Row 5: K12, k2tog, k29, ssk, k12.

Row 7: K11, k2tog, k29, ssk, k11.

Row 9: K10, k2tog, k29, ssk, k10.

Row 11: K9, k2tog, k29, ssk, k9.

49 sts rem. Work even in St st for 15 rows, end with a purl row about 7" (18 cm) from tip of heel. *Next row:* K23, k2tog, k24—48 sts rem.

Shape Toe:

Row 1: (RS) K9, k2tog, k2, ssk, k18, k2tog, k2, ssk, k9—44 sts.

Row 2 and all WS rows: P.

Row 3: K8, k2tog, k2, ssk, k16, k2tog, k2, ssk, k8—40 sts.

Row 5: K7, k2tog, k2, ssk, k14, k2tog, k2, ssk, k7—36 sts.

Cont to dec 4 sts every RS row in same manner until 16 sts rem, end on RS with row 15. From wrong side, sl first 4 sts to holder, sl next 8 sts to free needle; sl rem 4 sts to 2nd holder. From right side, beg with 4th st, sl 4 sts from first holder to 2nd needle; k4 sts from 2nd holder to same needle so that the open row edges are now at center of needle. Turn work, having points of both needles at right edge. Break yarn leaving a 14" (36 cm) end for weaving. Graft toe sts using Kitchener stitch (see Glossary, page 9). Work end in and fasten securely.

Snowman

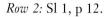

Snowman is worked in garter st (knit every row). With natural and smaller size straight needles, CO 9

sts. ***Bottom:*** K 1 row. Knit into front and back of first st at beg of each row until there are 17 sts. Knit even for 1" (2.5 cm). K2tog at beg of each row until 9 sts rem. ***Middle:*** Work same as bottom, inc to 13 sts and dec to 9 sts. ***Head:*** Work same as bottom, inc to 11 sts and dec to 7 sts. Bind off all sts.

Hat

With black, and smaller size needles, CO 11 sts. K 1 row, p 1 row, rep last 2 rows and bind off 2 sts at beg of each—7 sts. On RS with berry, k 1 row, p 1 row. With black, cont even for ¾" (2 cm). Bind off. Sew hat to snowman's head letting first 4 rows roll to the RS (see Finishing).

Scarf

With berry, and smaller size needles, make 2 pieces as follows: CO 18 sts. BO all sts. CO 14 sts. BO all sts. Sew one end to each side of neck, tie overlap knot in the center and stitch into place (see Finishing).

I-Cord

With berry, and smaller size needles, CO 3 sts for I-cord (see Glossary, page 8). Make about 42" (106.5 cm) in length.

Bobbles

With natural, make 40 bobbles. Using smaller size needles, CO 1 st leaving a 2" (5 cm) yarn tail. *Next row:* K1f, b&f—3 sts. Purl 1 row, knit 1 row, purl 1 row. *Next row:* Sl 1, k2tog, psso. Thread yarn through rem stitch and tie off. Cut yarn leaving a 2" (5 cm) tail.

Finishing

Place stocking on flat surface and position snowman. Stitch into place. Sew on hat and scarf pieces. With black yarn make French knots (see Glossary, page 9) for eyes, mouth, and the 3 body buttons. ***Carrot nose:*** With orange yarn, sew 2 diagonal lines side by side, then stitch across both lines in 3 different spots to represent ridges in a carrot. ***Arms:*** Using black yarn, make two "stick" arms as shown in photo. ***Snow bobbles:*** Thread yarn ends on a tapestry needle and insert needle to WS. Pull yarn through to WS, remove tapestry needle and tie yarn ends together, securing bobble to stocking. ***Close stocking seam:*** Sew edges of stocking together, from top to toe. At stocking top, turn hem to inside at turning ridge and stitch into place. Sew I-cord around top of cuff making a 3½" (9 cm) loop for hanger. Sew remaining I-cord around stocking about 3" (7.5 cm) down from the top. Weave in all ends.

Nicky Epstein has been a free-lance knitwear designer, teacher, and author for more than 20 years, with designs featured in numerous magazines, books, museum exhibitions, and television programs. Her books include Nicky Epstein's Knitted Embellishments *(Interweave Press, 1999).*

DIAMONDS IN THE ROUGH ARGYLE STOCKING

Jennifer Steinberg

DESIGNER JENNIFER STEINBERG TRANSLATES CLASSIC ARGYLE DIAMONDS INTO CHRISTMAS JEWELS IN THIS SURPRISINGLY EASY STOCKING WITH A TWEEDY, RUSTIC FEEL. THE ENTIRE STOCKING IS KNIT IN ONE PIECE ON STRAIGHT NEEDLES, WITH ONLY THE HEEL KNIT IN THE ROUND.

Finished Size

About 8" (20.5 cm) across top of stocking; 16" (40.5 cm) from top to heel; 12" (30.5 cm) from toe to heel.

Yarn

Heavy worsted weight, approximately 140 yd (128 m) gray; 100 yd (93 m) each red and green; 10 yd (9-10 m) each blue and gold.

Needles

Size 7 (4.5 mm): straight and double-pointed (dpn). Adjust needle size if necessary to obtain the correct gauge.

Notions

2 stitch holders; 5 bobbins; tapestry needle; 2 markers (m).

Gauge

18 sts and 28 rows = 4" (10 cm) in St st.

Note Two edge stitches (for seaming purposes) are picked up after placing 36 heel sts on holders (18 sts on each side of instep). Seam sts are not shown on chart, and are worked in gray either side of chart sts. They are eliminated during toe decreases.

LEG

With gray and straight needles, CO 71 sts. Work 3 rows in St st, end with a RS row. ***Next row:*** (WS) K1, *yo, k2tog; rep from * across row (picot point turning ridge). Work 4 rows in St st. Knit 1 row with red. Purl 1 row with green. Work in St st for 14 rows with gray. Knit 1 row with green. Purl 1 row with red. Join gray and follow Argyle patt chart Rows 1–106; after Row 70, place 18 sts at beg of next 2 rows on stitch holders—35 sts rem. Pick up one st each side of the sts on needle (for seaming) and work them in gray along with chart sts. ***Begin toe shaping:*** Work 1 row with gray. Work 4 rows in St st with red.

Row 1: K1, ssk, knit to last 3 sts, k2tog, k1.

Row 2: Purl.

Work last 2 rows three times—29 sts rem.

Next row: Rep dec row 1.

Next row: P1, p2tog, purl to last 3 sts, p2tog tbl, p1.

Rep last 2 rows until 9 sts rem on needle. Work 1 row in St st. Work increase rows as follows:

Row 1: K2, M1, knit to last 2 sts, M1, k2.

Row 2: P2, M1, purl to last 2 sts, M1, p2.

A
CHRISTMAS
CAROL
BROADUS

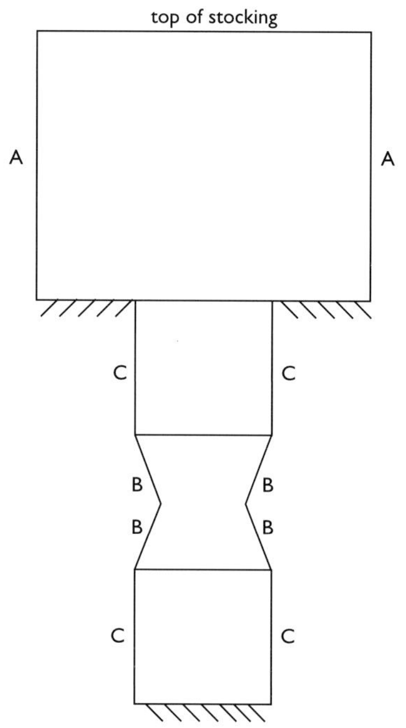

After knitting flat stocking and before knitting heel, seam as follows:

A. Back leg seam
B. Toe seams
C. Instep seams
/// indicates heel stitches

Rep last 2 rows until 29 sts are on needle.

Next row: Work 1 row in St st.

Next row: Work increase row 2.

Work last 2 rows three times—35 sts. Work 4 rows in St st. With gray, work 36 rows in St st. Place rem 35 sts on a stitch holder.

Heel

Thread yarn on tapestry needle and sew back leg seam and instep seams. Slip 35 leg stitches onto dpn so that the leg sts are divided evenly on 2 dpn, 18 sts on one needle, and 17 sts on another. You may have to increase a stitch or two in order to have sufficient number of sts after seaming the back leg. Place the 35 foot sts onto one dpn—70 sts. ***Heel decreases:***

Rnd 1: Beg with needle holding 35 foot sts, join red and knit one rnd.

Rnd 2: On needle #1, k1, ssk, knit to last 2 sts, k2tog. On needle #2, (18sts) k1, ssk, knit to end of needle. On needle #3, (17sts) knit to last 2 sts, k2tog.

Rnd 3: Knit.

Rep rnds 2 and 3 twice—58 sts. Work heel decrease rnd 2 every rnd 12 times or until a total of 10 sts rem. Arrange sts on 2 needles each with 5 sts. Graft heel sts together using Kitchener stitch (see Glossary, page 9).

Finishing

Cuff: Fold hem to inside of stocking at picot turning edge. Thread yarn on tapestry needle and sew hem to inside of stocking, making sure sewing stitches are not too tight, or visible from the public side. ***I-Cord hanger:*** With green yarn or color of your choice, make a 4 st I-cord (see Glossary, page 8) about 4" (10cm) in length. Fold I-cord in half and attach securely to stocking. Weave in all ends. If desired, put a name on top of the stocking in St st band using duplicate st (see Glossary, page 8, and alphabet chart, page 94). Block stocking.

Jennifer Weathersbee Steinberg is a college student who recently relocated from Philadelphia to Minneapolis. A self-taught knitter, she loves to create handmade knitwear for her husband and their Boston terrier, Daisy.

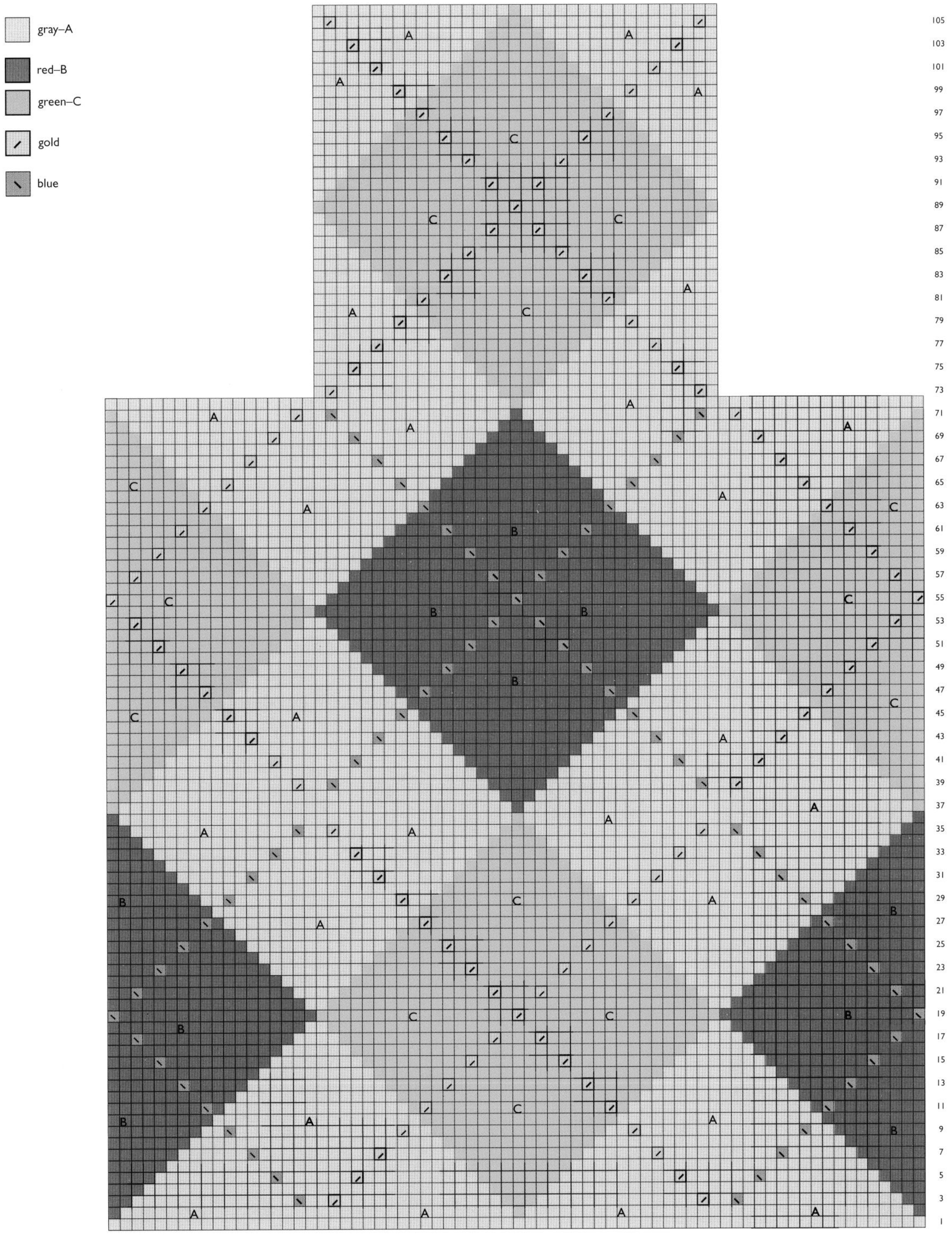

Argyle Pattern Chart

VILLAGE OF KIRBLA ESTONIAN STOCKING

Nancy Bush

This design was inspired by a knitted nineteenth-century sock from the village of Kirbla, now in the collection of the Estonian National Museum in Tartu, Estonia. The original stocking is quite long, with the stripe pattern the full length of the sock. Substitute more traditional Christmas colors, if you prefer, for Nancy's festive greens and gold.

Finished Size
About 7" (18 cm) wide and 12" (30.5 cm) long before blocking.

Yarn
Sport weight yarn, approximately 150 yd (137 m) dark green; 60 yd (55 m) each natural and gold; 40 yd (37 m) apple green.

Needles
Size 3 (3.25 mm): set of 5 double-pointed needles (dpn); size 2: (2.75 mm) set of 5 dpn.

Gauge
24 sts and 28 rounds = 4" (10 cm) in cir, patterned St st before blocking.

Notions
Tapestry needle; markers.

Note When instructions specify increases or decreases, they should be evenly spaced within the rnd indicated.

Leg

With smaller needles and green, CO 88 sts, leaving about 12" (31 cm) of tail from this cast-on for making the hanger loop later. Divide sts onto 4 dpn needles (22 sts on each needle) and join, being careful not to twist sts. This join is the "seam line" and marks the beginning of all future rounds.

Cuff: Purl 1 rnd. Work in k2, p2 rib for 5 rounds. Purl 1 rnd. *Next rnd:* *K2 tog, yo; rep from * to end of rnd. Knit 1 Rnd. Purl 1 rnd. Change to larger needles and knit one rnd. Follow Leg chart Rnds 1 through 81, increasing and decreasing where indicated on chart. Leg measures 12 inches (30.5 cm). Adjust stitches as follows: 16 sts on needle #1, 20 on needle #2 and needle #3, and 16 sts on needle #4 — 72 sts.

Heel

With green, k across 16 sts on needle #1. Turn, sl 1, p 31. These 32 sts form the heel flap. Hold rem 40 sts for instep. ***Heel flap:*** Heel flap is worked back and forth in rows.

Row 1: Sl 1, k31.

Row 2: Sl 1, p31.

Repeat above 2 rows for a total of 20 rows. End with row 2 (WS).

Turn heel:

Row 1: K20, ssk, turn.

Row 2: Sl 1, p8, p2tog, turn.

Row 3: Sl 1, k8, ssk, turn.

Row 4: Sl 1, p8, p2tog, turn.

Repeat Rows 3 and 4 until all heel

sts are worked—10 heel sts rem.

Foot

Gusset: Continuing with green, k across the 10 heel sts. Pick up and k10 sts along right side of heel flap. Work 40 instep sts. With an empty needle, pick up and k10 sts along left side of heel flap—70 sts. K5 sts to center of heel, pm for beg of rnd. Continue following Foot chart as established, decreasing where indicated. When you have completed the third striped pattern on foot (60 sts), adjust stitches to 15 on each needle.

Shape toe:

Rnd 1: With green, work 1 rnd even.

Rnd 2: Knit tog the last 2 sts on each needle—56 sts.

Rnd 3: Knit.

Rnd 4: *K6, k2tog; rep from *to end of rnd—49 sts.

Rnd 5: Knit.

Rnd 6: *K5, k2tog; rep from * to end of rnd—42 sts.

Rnd 7: Knit.

Rnd 8: *K4, k2tog; rep from * to end of rnd—35 sts.

Rnd 9: Knit.

Rnd 10: *K3, k2tog; rep from * to end of rnd—28 sts.

Rnd 11: Knit.

Rnd 12: *K2, k2tog; rep from * to end of rnd—21 sts.

Rnd 13: *K1, k2tog; rep from * to end of rnd—14 sts.

Rnd 14: *K2tog; rep from * to end of rnd—7 sts rem.

Break yarn, thread tail through sts, pull snug, and fasten off.

Finishing

Using tail remaining from cast-on, and adding one 12" (30.5 cm) strand of green and 2 strands each of gold and natural, make a "braid" as follows: Divide ends into 2 groups of 3 threads each, one of each color. Now twist the two groups between your fingers to the RIGHT and then wrap the two groups of threads over each other to the LEFT. Continue until you have a twisted cord about 4" (10 cm) long. Secure the ends by making an overhand knot at the end. Fold cord and attach securely inside the cuff edge. Weave in all ends. Block stocking lightly.

Nancy Bush is a writer, designer, teacher, and the owner of Wooly West, a mail-order yarn business in Salt Lake City. She's interested in and inspired by the knitting traditions of Northern Europe, especially Estonia. Nancy is the author of Folk Socks: History and Techniques of Handknitted Footwear *(Interweave Press, 1994), and* Folk Knitting in Estonia: A Garland of Symbolism, Tradition, and Technique *(Interweave Press, 1999). Her newest book is* Knitting on the Road: Sock Patterns for the Traveling Knitter *(Interweave Press, 2001).*

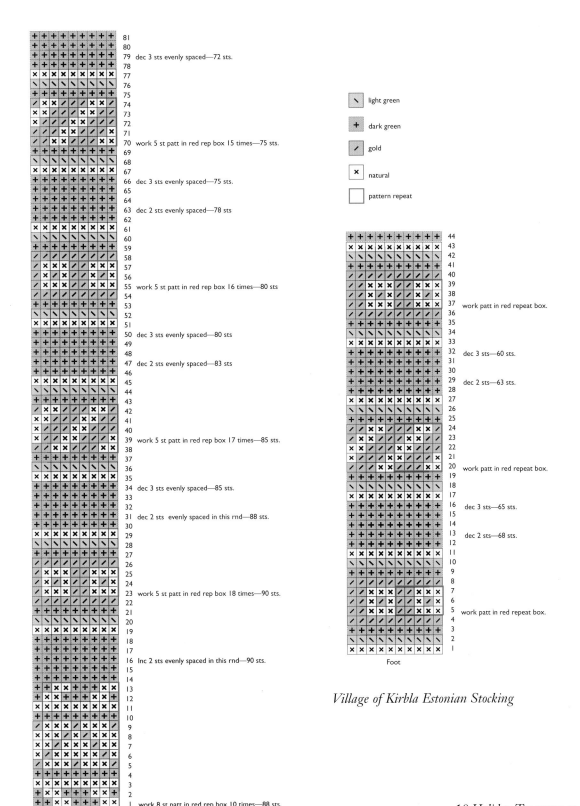

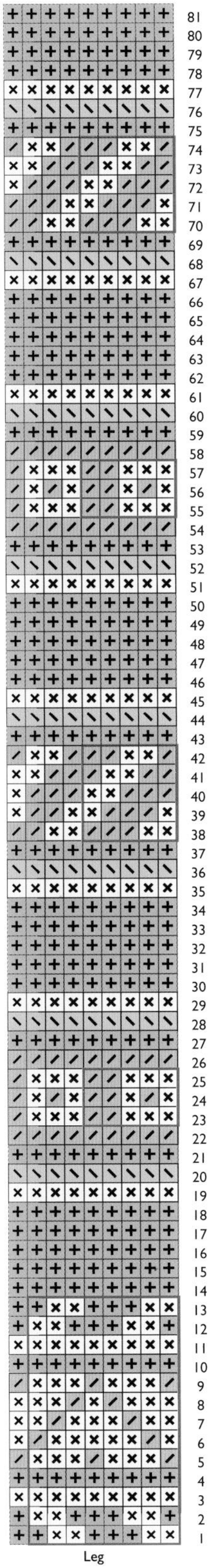
79 dec 3 sts evenly spaced—72 sts.
70 work 5 st patt in red rep box 15 times—75 sts.
66 dec 3 sts evenly spaced—75 sts.
63 dec 2 sts evenly spaced—78 sts
55 work 5 st patt in red rep box 16 times—80 sts
50 dec 3 sts evenly spaced—80 sts
47 dec 2 sts evenly spaced—83 sts
39 work 5 st patt in red rep box 17 times—85 sts.
34 dec 3 sts evenly spaced—85 sts.
31 dec 2 sts evenly spaced in this rnd—88 sts.
23 work 5 st patt in red rep box 18 times—90 sts.
16 Inc 2 sts evenly spaced in this rnd—90 sts.
1 work 8 st patt in red rep box 10 times—88 sts.
Leg

light green
dark green
gold
natural
pattern repeat

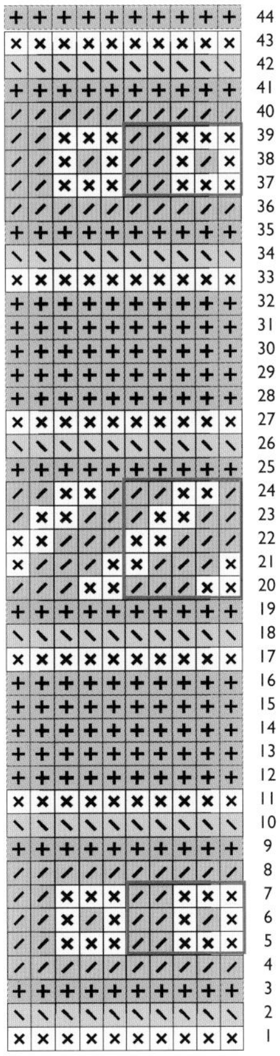
37 work patt in red repeat box.
32 dec 3 sts—60 sts.
29 dec 2 sts—63 sts.
20 work patt in red repeat box.
16 dec 3 sts—65 sts.
13 dec 2 sts—68 sts.
5 work patt in red repeat box.
Foot

Village of Kirbla Estonian Stocking

A FETCHING STOCKING

Kathy Brklacich Sasser

DESIGNED ESPECIALLY FOR YOUR BEST CANINE FRIEND, THIS PROJECT WILL CHALLENGE YOUR INTARSIA KNITTING SKILLS (OR DUPLICATE STITCH, IF YOU PREFER). WORK THE HOLLY BERRIES THAT ADORN THE DOG'S BONE IN FRENCH KNOTS TO ADD DIMENSION.

Finished Size
About 6¼" (16 cm) across top of stocking; about 19" (48 cm) long.

Yarn
Heavy worsted weight yarn, approximately 130 yd (119 m) dark red; 130 yd (119 m) tan; 85 yd (78 m) green; 65 yd (60 m) brown.

Needles
Size 8 (5.0 mm): 10" (25 cm) straight or 24" (61 cm) circular, and double-pointed needles (dpn). Adjust needle size if necessary to obtain the correct gauge.

Notions
Stitch holders (3); tapestry needle.

Gauge
18 sts and 24 rows = 4" (10 cm) in St st.

Note Motifs may be worked using the intarsia method or added later with duplicate stitch (see Glossary, pages 7 and 8).

STITCH

Seed Stitch:

Row 1: *K1, P1; rep from*

Following Rows: Knit the purl sts and purl the knit sts as they face you.

LEG

With green, CO 64 sts loosely, work 22 rows in seed st. Changing colors as indicated, follow chart, Rows 1 through 94. Read RS (odd-numbered) rows right to left, and WS rows left to right. ***Shape Instep at row 57:*** (RS) With tan, knit across 16 sts (first half of heel), place these 16 sts on holder. Follow chart across center 32 sts (instep). Do not cut yarn. With tan knit across last 16 sts. Cut yarn and place these 16 sts on another holder (second half of heel). Rejoin tan at instep (WS), and continue to follow chart for instep through Row 94, ending with a purl row. Cut yarn and place instep sts on a third holder.

HEEL

Slip first and last 16 sts from holders onto one dpn needle, making the center seam line at the center of the needle—32 sts.

Row 1: (WS) With tan, sl 1, p31.

Row 2: *Sl 1, k1, rep from * across.

Repeat these two rows for 2½" (6.5 cm) ending with a WS row.

Turn heel:

Row 1: (RS) Sl 1, k17, ssk, k1, turn.

Row 2: Sl 1, p5, p2tog, p1, turn.

Row 3: Sl 1, k6, ssk, k1, turn.

Row 4: Sl 1, p7, p2tog, p1, turn.

Cont in this manner, working one more stitch before the dec on each row until all sts have been worked, ending with a WS row—18 sts. The

last two rows will end after the decrease. Cut yarn.

Foot

Gusset: Worked back and forth in rows. With RS facing join red, and working with two dpn, pick up 12 sts along side of heel, then knit 9 heel sts onto same needle. With another dpn k across last 9 heel sts and pick up 12 sts along other side of heel—42 sts. Turn and purl one row across sts on both needles.

Row 1: (RS) K1, ssk, knit across sts on first needle then knit to last 3 sts on second dpn, k2tog, k1. Turn.

Row 2: Purl.

Repeat last two rows until 28 sts rem (14 sts on each dpn). Work even until sole section measures same length as instep, ending with a knit row. Cut yarn. Divide sts as follows: The last 14 sts worked are needle #1. Slip the 32 instep sts on another dpn (needle #2). The remaining 14 sts are needle #3—60 sts. Sew sides of instep to heel. Join green at beginning of needle #1 and knit across this needle. On needle #2, k1, ssk, knit to last 3 sts, k2 tog, k1. Knit across needle #3—58 sts. Join cir and work 7 rnds in seed st. Cut yarn.

Toe shaping: With red, knit across needle #1. On needle #2, k1, ssk, knit to last 3 sts, k2tog, k1. Knit across needle #3—56 sts.

Rnd 1: Knit even.

Rnd 2: Knit to last 3 sts on needle #1, k2tog, k1. On needle #2, k1, ssk, knit to last 3 sts, k2tog, k1. On needle #3, k1, ssk, knit to end.

Rep last two rnds until 32 sts rem. Knit 1 rnd even.

Finishing

Graft toe sts together using Kitchener stitch (see Glossary, page 9). ***I-cord hanger:*** With dpn and green, CO 4 sts and work I-cord (see Glossary, page 8) for 5½" (14 cm). With yarn threaded on tapestry needle, weave through all sts to secure, and imbed yarn tail in center of I-cord. Sew back seams of stocking, matching all color sections. Fold top seed st section in half and sew in place. Weave in all loose ends. Fold I-cord in half and sew in place along seam line on the inside of stocking. Block if necessary.

Kathy Sasser owns and operates Arky Arky Creations. A former yarn store owner and a certified Master Knitter, her articles and designs have appeared in magazines and books including Knitting Digest, INKnitters, Knitters, *and* Cast On. *Kathy is an executive board member of the International Network for Knitters and formerly served as co-chair of The Knitting Guild of America's Master Hand Knitting Committee.*

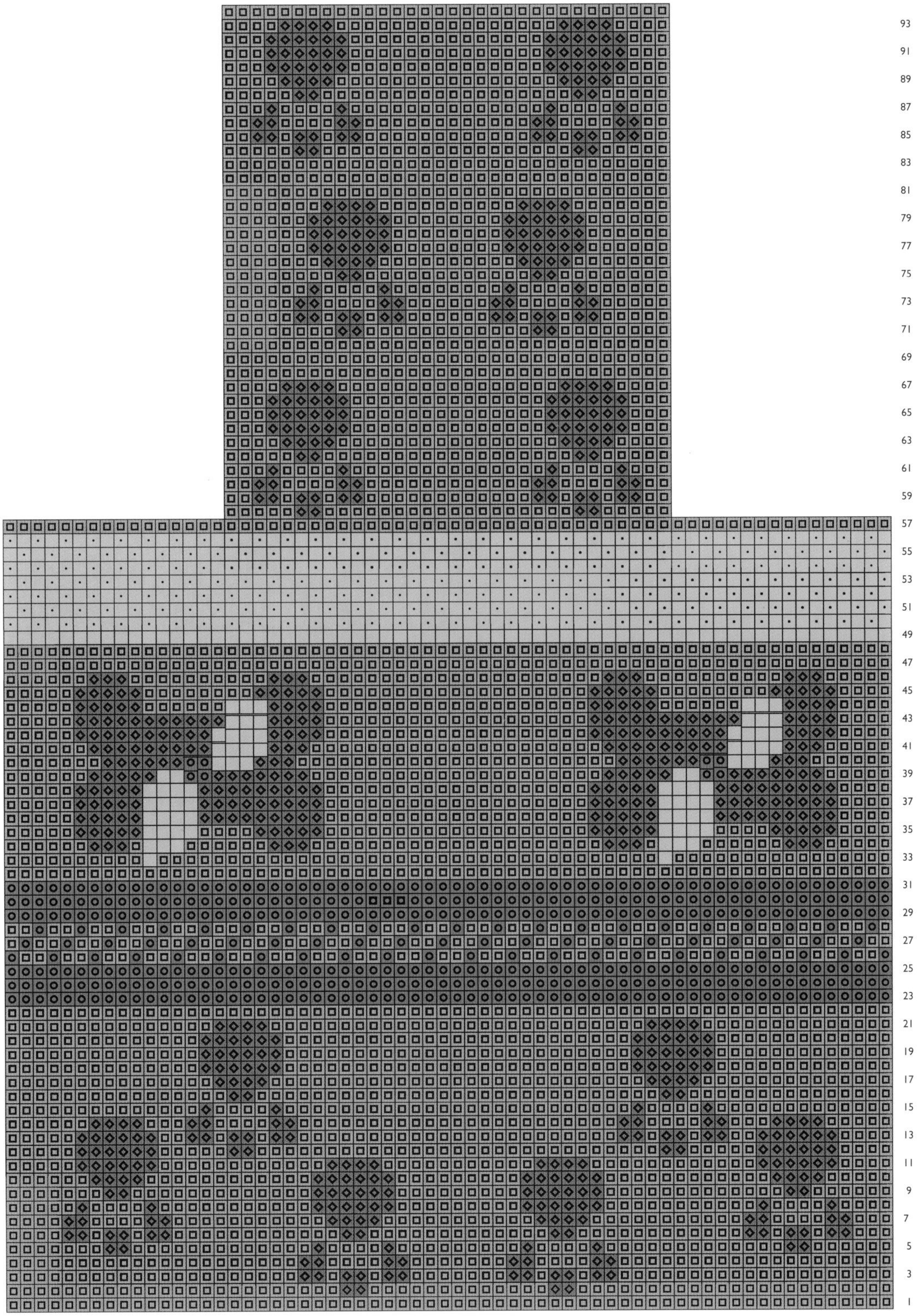

green: purl on RS; knit on WS.

green: knit on RS; purl on WS.

red: knit on RS; purl on WS.

brown: knit on RS; purl on WS.

tan: knit on RS; purl on WS.

A Fetching Stocking

COUNTERPANE AND LACE STOCKING

Susan Strawn Bailey

A vintage Victorian counterpane bedspread inspired Susan Strawn Bailey to design this graceful, lovely stocking. An eight-stitch razor shell lace cuff suggests the counterpane's traditional lacy border. Although the counterpane pattern looks complex, it consists of eight identical squares with an engaging but not especially difficult series of bobbles, yarnovers, and leaf shapes made with increases and decreases. The simple garter stitch heel and stockinette foot knit up quickly.

Finished Size
About 6½" (16.5 cm) across top of stocking; 15½" (39.5 cm) from top of cuff to toe.

Yarn
Sport weight yarn, approximately 200 yards (183 m) autumnal red (MC); 100 yards (93 m) parchment (CC). We used a cotton blend to echo the look of a vintage counterpane.

Needles
Size 4 (3.5 mm): 10" (26 cm) straight needles, set of 5 double-pointed needles (dpn). Adjust needle size if necessary to obtain the correct gauge.

Notions
Stitch holder; tapestry needle.

Gauge
26 sts and 36 rows = 4" (10 cm) in St st.

Stitches

Make Bobble:

Row 1: Make 3 sts from one by working k1, p1, k1 into same st, turn.

Row 2: Sl 1, p2, turn.

Row 3: Sl 1, k2, turn.

Row 4: Sl 1, p2, turn.

Row 5: Sl 1, k2tog tbl, psso.

Leg

Counterpane Squares: Make 8 squares. With MC and straight needles, CO 1 st. K1, p1, k1 into the CO st—3 sts.

Row 1: (RS) Knit in front and back of first st, yo, k1, yo, k1—6 sts.

Row 2: Sl 1 purlwise, yo, p5—7 sts.

Row 3: Sl 1 knitwise, yo, k2, yo, k1, yo, k3—10 sts.

Row 4: Sl 1, yo, k1, p5, k2, p1—11 sts.

Row 5: Sl 1, yo, k4, yo, k1, yo, k5—14 sts.

Row 6: Sl 1, yo, k2, p7, k3, p1—15 sts.

Row 7: Sl 1, yo, k6, yo, k1, yo, k7—18 sts.

Row 8: Sl 1, yo, k3, p9, k4, p1—19 sts.

Row 9: Sl 1, yo, k4, sl 1, k1, psso, k5, k2tog, k5—18 sts.

Row 10: Sl 1, yo, k4, p7, k5, p1—19 sts.

Row 11: Sl 1, yo, k5, sl 1, k1, psso, k3, k2tog, k6—18 sts.

Row 12: Sl 1, yo, k5, p5, k6, p1—19 sts.

Row 13: Sl 1, yo, k6, sl 1, k1, psso, k1, k2tog, k7—18 sts.

Row 14: Sl 1, yo, k6, p3, k7, p1—19 sts.

Row 15: Sl 1, yo k7, sl 1, k2tog, psso, k8—18 sts.

Row 16: Sl 1, yo, p17—19 sts.

Row 17: Sl 1, yo, k18—20 sts.

Row 18: Sl 1, yo, k18, p1—21 sts.

Row 19: Sl 1, yo, *k2tog, yo; rep from* 8 times, k2—22 sts.

Row 20: Sl 1, yo, k20, p1—23 sts.

Row 21: Sl 1, yo, k22—24 sts.

Row 22: Sl 1, yo, p23—25 sts.

Row 23: Sl 1, yo, k1, *make bobble (MB), k2; rep from * 6 times, k2—26 sts.

Row 24: Sl 1, p25—26 sts.

Row 25: Sl 1, sl 1, k1, psso, k23—25 sts.

Row 26: Sl 1, k2tog, k21, p1—24 sts.

Row 27: Sl 1, sl 1, k1, psso, *yo, k2tog; rep from * 9 times, k1—23 sts.

Row 28: Sl 1, K2tog, K19, P1—22 sts.

Row 29: Sl 1, sl 1, k1, psso, k19—21 sts.

Row 30: Sl 1, p2tog, p18—20 sts.

Row 31: Sl 1, sl 1, k1, psso, k17—19 sts.

Row 32: Sl 1, k2tog, k15, p1—18 sts.

Row 33: Sl 1, sl 1, k1, psso, k15—17sts.

Row 34: Sl 1, k2tog, k13, p1—16 sts.

Row 35: Sl 1, sl 1, k1, psso, k5, MB, k7—15 sts.

Row 36: Sl 1, k2tog, k11, p1—14 sts.

Row 37: Sl 1, sl 1, k1, psso, k2, *MB, k1; rep from * 2 times, k3—13 sts.

Row 38: Sl 1, k2tog, k9, p1—12 sts.

Row 39: Sl 1, sl 1, k1, psso, k3, MB, k5—11 sts.

Row 40: Sl 1, k2tog, k7, p1—10 sts.

Row 41: Sl 1, sl 1, k1, psso, k7—9 sts.

Row 42: Sl 1, k2tog, k5, p1—8 sts.

Row 43: Sl 1, sl 1, k1, psso, k5—7 sts.

Row 44: Sl 1, k2tog, k3, p1—6 sts.

Row 45: Sl 1, sl 1, k1, psso, k3—5 sts.

Row 46: Sl 1, k2tog, k1, p1—4 sts.

Row 47: Sl 1, sl 1, k2tog, psso—2 sts.

Row 48: K2tog—1 st.

Draw yarn through loop.

With a tapestry needle, sew counterpane squares together. Align squares together so that the leaf motifs are at the centers. Stitch upper and lower squares together horizontally. Then stitch the 4 sections together vertically, making one large square. Rep with other 4 sections to make a second large square. Sew both squares together vertically, forming a tube. ***Cuff:*** With CC and right side facing, pick up and knit 96 sts in front and back of loops around top of stocking. Turn stocking to WS so that RS of cuff will face outwards when folded over. Knit cir for 3 inches. Purl 1 round for turning edge. Change to border pattern for 3½" (9 cm).
Lace Border: (Barbara Walker, *A Treasury of Knitting Patterns*)

Rnd 1 and all odd rnds: Knit.

Rnd 2: *YO, k2, sl 1, k2tog, psso, k2, yo, k1, repeat from *.

Bind off following an odd round. Weave in loose ends with tapestry needle.

Heel

With four dpn, pick up and knit 80 sts around lower edge of counterpane squares, beginning at a seam at the middle of the stocking. Knitting into the front and back of alternate loops will give you 80 sts. ***Heel flap:*** On the 4th and 1st needle, work across 42 sts and place them onto a stitch holder. Knit across 38 sts. Cont knitting in garter st across the 38 sts only for 3" (7.5 cm). On both sides of heel work edge loops as follows: At beg of row, k1tbl and at end of row slip the last st purlwise keeping yarn at front of work.

Turn heel: Work in garter st with decorative decrease.
Row 1: (RS) K22, sl 1, k1, psso, turn.

Row 2: Sl 1 purlwise, k7, p2tog, turn.

Row 3: Sl 1 knitwise, k7, sl 1, k1, psso, turn.

Row 4: Sl 1, k7, p2tog, turn.

Row 5: Sl 1, k7, sl 1, k1, psso, turn.

Cont to work back and forth as above, dec 1 st each row until 10 sts rem.

Row 29: (RS) K5, place marker to mark beg of gusset rnds.

Foot

Gusset: With needle #1, k5 across second half of heel sts, pick up and k12 in loops along side of heel flap. With needle #2, k42 across instep. With needle #3, pick up and k12 in loops along side other side of heel, k5 across first half of heel sts to beg marker—76 sts. Join into cir and beg shaping.

Rnd 1: Knit.

Rnd 2: Work to last 2 sts on needle #1 and k2tog. Knit across 42 instep sts on needle #2. On needle #3, ssk, knit to end of rnd.

Work last 2 rnds 6 times—64 sts rem. Knit for 3" (7.5 cm) or desired length, dec 1 st on last row—63 sts.

Shape Toe:

*Sl 1, k1, psso, k5, repeat from * around toe—54 sts.

Knit 4 rounds.

*Sl 1, k1, psso, k4, repeat from * around—45 sts.

Knit 3 rounds.

*Sl 1, k1, psso, k3, repeat from * around—36 sts.

Knit 2 rounds.

*Sl 1, k1, psso, k2, repeat from * around—27 sts.

Knit 1 round.

*Sl 1, k1, psso, k1, repeat from * around—18 sts.

*Sl 1, k1, psso, repeat from * around—9 sts.

Finishing

Cut yarn, leaving an 8" (20 cm) tail. Thread through a tapestry needle and draw through remaining loops twice. Pull thread gently to close toe opening and weave in ends. ***Hanger Loop:*** Make I-cord (see Glossary, page 8) about 4" (10 cm) long. Stitch to inside back of stocking.

Susan Strawn Bailey is an illustrator and photo stylist for Interweave Press. An ardent knitter since childhood, she collects vintage knitting and writes about knitting and other textile traditions.

HUGS AND KISSES ARAN STOCKING

Dee Lockwood

Designer Dee Lockwood's Aran-inspired stocking features a three-dimensional cable that reminds her of the Xs and Os used on Christmas cards to represent hugs and kisses. The latticed spindle design on the sides, she says, looks like the beautiful glass ornaments she remembers from childhood. For easier knitting, put each pattern on a separate needle.

Finished Size
About 5½" (14 cm) across top of stocking; 14¾" (37.5 cm) from cuff to bottom of heel; 10¾" (27 cm) from heel to toe.

Yarn
Worsted weight yarn, approximately 210 yd (190 m) white (color A); 90 yd (83 m) dark olive (color B).

Needles
Size 5 (3.75 mm) and size 6 (4.25 mm): sets of 5 double-pointed needles (dpn). Adjust needle sizes if necessary to obtain the correct gauge.

Notions
Markers (m); cable needle; tapestry needle.

Gauge 20 sts and 28 rows = 4" (10 cm) in St st on smaller needles.

ABBREVIATIONS

Kt: Knit second stitch on left needle, do not remove stitch, k first stitch on left needle, and remove both stitches.

2/2KRC: Sl next two stitches onto cable needle, hold in back, k2, k2 from cable needle.

2/2KLC: Sl next two stitches onto cable needle, hold in front, k2, k2 from cable needle.

2/2PRC: Sl next two stitches onto cable needle, hold in back, k2, p2 from cable needle.

2/2PLC: Sl next two stitches onto cable needle, hold in front, p2, k2 from cable needle.

2/1PRC: Sl next stitch onto cable needle, hold in back, k2, p1 from cable needle.

2/1PLC: Sl next two stitches onto cable needle, hold in front, p1, k2 from cable needle.

Right 1k/1p: Sl next stitch onto cable needle, hold in back, k1, p1 from cable needle.

Left 1k/1p: Sl next stitch onto cable needle, hold in front, p1, k1 from cable needle.

Stitches

OXOX Cable (Pattern A):
(Barbara Walker, *A Treasury of Knitting Patterns*)
(22 sts)

Rnd 1 and all odd rnds: K2, p1, k2, p2, k8, p2, k2, p1, k2.

Rnd 2: Kt, p1, kt, p2, k8, p2, kt, p1, kt.

Rnd 4: Kt, p1, kt, p2, 2/2KRC, 2/2KLC, p2, kt, p1, kt.

Rnd 6: Kt, p1, kt, p2, k8, p2, kt, p1, kt.

Rnd 8: Kt, p1, kt, p2, 2/2KLC, 2/2KRC, p2, kt, p1, kt.

Rnd 10: Repeat row 6.

Rnd 12: Repeat row 8.

Rnd 14: Repeat row 2.

Rnd 16: Repeat row 4.

Latticed Spindle (Pattern B):
(Barbara Walker, *Charted Knitting Designs, A Third Treasury of Knitting Patterns*)
(24 sts increasing to 28 sts)

Rnds 1 through 4: P10, k4, p10.

Rnd 5: P10, M1, k4, M1, p10—26 sts.

Rnd 6: P10, k6, p10.

Rnd 7: P10, k1, M1, k4, M1, k1, p10—28 sts.

Rnd 8: P10, k8, p10.

Rnd 9: P8, 2/2PRC, k4, 2/2PLC, p8.

Rnd 10: P8, k2, p2, k4, p2, k2, p8.

Rnd 11: P6, 2/2PRC, p1, 2/1PRC, 2/1PLC, p1, 2/2PLC, p6.

Rnd 12: P6, k2, p3, k2, p2, k2, p3, k2, p6.

Rnd 13: P4, 2/2PRC, p2, 2/1PRC, p2, 2/1PLC, p2, 2/2PLC, p4.

Rnds 14 to 16: [P4, k2] 4 times, p4.

Rnd 17: P3, [right 1k/1p, left 1k/1p, p2] 4 times, p1.

Rnd 18: P3, [k1, p2] 8 times, p1.

Rnd 19: P2, [right 1k/1p, p2, left 1k/1p] 4 times, p2.

Rnd 20: P2, k1, [p4, k2] 3 times, p4, k1, p2.

Rnd 21: P2, k1, [p4, kt] 3 times, p4, k1, p2.

Rnd 22: Same as row 20.

Rnd 23: P2, [left 1k/1p, p2, right 1k/1p] 4 times, p2.

Rnd 24: P3, [k1, p2] 8 times, p1.

Rnd 25: P3, [left 1k/1p, right 1k/1p, p2] 4 times, p1.

Rnds 26 to 28: [P4, k2] 4 times, p4.

Rnd 29: P4, 2/2PLC, p2, 2/1PLC, p2, 2/1PRC, p2, 2/2PRC, p4.

Rnd 30: P6, k2, p3, k2, p2, k2, p3, k2, p6.

Rnd 31: P6, 2/2PLC, p1, 2/1PLC, 2/1PRC, p1, 2/2PRC, p6.

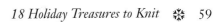

Rnd 32: P8, k2, p2, k4, p2, k2, p8.

Rnd 33: P8, 2/2PLC, k4, 2/2PRC, p8.

Rnd 34: P10, k8, p10.

Rnd 35: P10, k1, k2tog, k2, ssk, k1, p10—26 sts.

Rnd 36: P10, k6, p10.

Rnd 37: P10, k2tog, k2, ssk, p10—24 sts.

Rnd 38: P10, k4, p10.

Cuff

With color B and larger needles, CO 88 sts. Divide among 4 needles. Join work being careful not to twist. Place marker at beginning of round. Work in k2, p2 ribbing until piece measures 3" (7.5 cm). Purl one round. Change to color A and smaller needles. Purl one round.

Leg

Set up row: On needle #1, k2, p2tog, k2, p2, k1, M1, k4, M1, k1, p2, k2, p2tog, k2—22 sts. On needle #2, p10, k1, M1, k1, M1, p10—24 sts. On needle #3, same as needle #1. On needle #4, same as needle #2—92 sts total.

Work patt A on needles #1 and #3. Work patt B on needles #2 and #4. Cont until you have completed two repetitions of patt B, then work rows 1 and 2 of patt B.

Heel

Heel flap:

Set up row: On needle #1, cont patt A. On needle #2, p10, k4, p10. On needle #3, cont patt A. P10, k4 from needle #4 onto needle #3. Transfer previous 50 sts onto stitch holder—42 sts on needles for heel flap. Change to color B. Work back and forth in the following pattern:

Row 1: (RS) K10, pm, cont working even-numbered rows of patt A over next 22 sts, pm, k10.

Row 2: (WS) Sl 1, p7, k2, p2, k1, p2, k2, p8, k2, p2, k1, p2, k2, p8.

Row 3: [Sl 1, k1] 4 times, p2, sl m, cont working even-numbered rows of patt A over next 22 sts, sl m, p2, [sl 1, k1] 4 times.

Rep rows 2 and 3 until you have worked 22 rows ending with row 2.

Heel cap:

Row 1: (RS) [Sl 1, k1] 4 times, p2, cont working even-numbered rows of patt A over next 22 sts, sl 1, k1, psso, turn.

Row 2: (WS) Sl 1, p2, k1, p2, k2, p8, k2, p2, k1, p2, p2tog, turn.

Row 3: Sl 1 knitwise, cont working even-numbered rows of patt A over next 22 sts, sl 1, k1, psso, turn.

Rep rows 2 and 3 until 24 sts remain, ending with row 2.

Row 4: Sl 1 knitwise, continue patt A over next 22 sts, k1.

Row 5: P2tog, p1, k1, p2, k2, p8, k2, p2, k1, p1, p2tog—22sts.

Foot

Instep Decreases:

Change to Color A.

Set up rnd: (RS) On needle #1, cont working patt A across 22 sts. On needle #2, pick up 13 sts along side of heel flap, k4, p10 from sts held on stitch holder. On needle #3, cont working patt A across next 22 sts from stitch holder. ***Note:*** You may not be on the same row of patt A for needles #1 and #3. On needle #4, from stitch holder p10, k4, pick up 13 sts along side of heel flap—98 sts total. You should now have 22 sts on needles #1 and #3, and 27 sts on needles #2 and #4.

Rnd 1: Cont working patt A on needles #1 and #3. On needle #2, p10, k2tog, k5, p10. On needle #4, p10, k5, ssk, p10—96 sts.

Rnd 2: Cont working patt A on needles #1 and #3. On needle #2, p10, k6, p10. On needle #4, p10, k6, p10.

Rnd 3: Cont working patt A on needles #1 and #3. On needle #2, p10, k2tog, k4, p10. On needle #4, p10, k4, ssk, p10—94 sts.

Rnd 4: Cont working patt A on needles #1 and #3. On needle #2, p10, k5, p10. On needle 4, p10, k5, p10.

Rnd 5: Cont working patt A on needles #1 and #3. On needle #2, p10, k2tog, k3, p10. On needle #4, p10, k3, ssk, p10—92 sts.

Rnd 6: Cont working patt A on needles #1 and #3. On needle #2, p10, k4, p10. On needle #4, p10, k4, p10.

Cont to work patt A on needles #1 and #3. Work patt B on needles #2 and #4. Cont until you have completed one repetition of patt B.

Toe

Change to color B. For all rows on the toe, cont patt A as established on needles #1 and #3. Follow pattern below for needles #2 and #4.

Set up rnd: Knit.

Rnd 1: K1, ssk, p7, k4, p7, k2tog, k1 (22 sts on each needle).

Rnd 2: K2, p7, k4, p7, k2.

Rnd 3: K1, ssk, p6, k4, p6, k2tog, k1 (20 sts on each needle).

Rnd 4: K2, p6, k4, p6, k2.

Rnd 5: K1, ssk, p5, k4, p5, k2tog, k1 (18 sts on each needle).

Rnd 6: K2, p5, k4, p5, k2.

Rnd 7: K1, ssk, p4, k4, p4, k2tog, k1 (16 sts on each needle).

Rnd 8: K2, p4, k4, p4, k2.

Rnd 9: K1, ssk, p3, k4, p3, k2tog, k1 (14 sts on each needle).

Rnd 10: K2, p3, k4, p3, k2.

Rnd 11: K1, ssk, p2, k4, p2, k2tog, k1 (12 sts on each needle).

Rnd 12: K1, ssk, p1, k4, p1, k2tog, k1 (10 sts on each needle).

Rnd 13: K1, ssk, k4, k2tog, k1 (8 sts on each needle).

Rnd 14: K1, ssk, k2, k2tog, k1 (6 sts on each needle).

Rnd 15: K1, ssk, k2tog, k1 (4 sts on each needle).

Rnd 16: Ssk, k2tog (2 sts on each needle).

Rnd 17: Ssk (1 st on each needle).

Finishing

Use Kitchener stitch (see Glossary, page 9) to graft together rem sts. ***Loop:*** CO 4 sts with color B and knit I-cord (see Glossary, page 8) for about 8" (20.5 cm). Cut yarn leaving 18"(45.5 cm) tail. Thread yarn on tapestry needle and weave through sts, pull gently and close sts. Using same yarn, fold I-cord in half and attach approximately 2" (5 cm) from top on inside of stocking at center back.

Dee Lockwood, Controller for Interweave Press, has been knitting since her college days in the 1960s; her teacher was a fellow student. "Since then I have managed to learn something from every knitter I've encountered," she says.

NAUGHTY BUT NICE VICTORIAN ELEGANCE

Sasha Kagan

A visit to the historic "House of Joy" in Jerome, Arizona, reputed to be the roughest, toughest town in the West in Victorian days, inspired Sasha Kagan to create this unconventional stocking. "Under the prim Victorian matron's staid exterior, there was the elegant and slightly shocking stocking—a gesture toward the emancipation of women," Kagan says. "I like to think that at Christmas, the stocking would be filled with perfumes, soaps, and other womanly extravagances." Make this stocking for any smart, sexy lady, or for a Victorian parlor.

Finished Size
About 5"(13cm) across top of stocking 19½" (49.5 cm) from cuff to heel; 10" (25.5 cm) from heel to toe.

Yarn
2-ply fingering weight wool, approximately 280 yd (256 m) black (MC); 50 yd (46 m) each lilac, bluebell, pale pink, mid pink, crimson, teal, mauve, purple;10 yd (9.15 m) each magenta and taupe.

Needles
Cuff—Size 0 (2mm); Size C (3mm) crochet hook.
Stocking—Size 2 (2.75 mm): straight and set of 4 double-pointed needles (dpn). Adjust needle size if necessary to obtain the correct gauge.

Notions
Bobbins optional; tapestry needle.

Gauge
31 sts and 38 rows = 4" (10cm) in St st on larger needles.

Note Work intarsia motifs with short lengths of yarn (use bobbins or leave yarn hanging). Weave the background color along behind each motif, catching it in on every other stitch.

Stitches
Seed Stitch:

Row 1: *K1, p1, rep from * around.

Next rows: Knit the purl sts and purl the knit sts.

Leg

Cuff: With MC and smaller needles, CO 78 sts. Work 12 rows Seed st. Change to larger needles and follow Chart A from row 1 to row 102. Repeat small flower motif pattern again from row 47 to row 84, then prepare for heel.

CHANDON

Heel

Heel flap: Change to dpn. Place center back 38 sts (19 from each side) onto one needle to work heel flap, working k2tog over gap (37 sts). Divide 40 instep sts onto 2 needles or place on holders temporarily.

Row 1: (WS) Sl 1, p36.

Row 2: *Sl 1, k1; rep from * to row end.

Repeat these two rows 14 times, then work row 1 again—31 rows.

Turn heel:

Row 1: (RS) Sl 1, k21, ssk, k1, turn.

Row 2: Sl 1, p6, p2tog, p1, turn.

Row 3: Sl 1, k7, ssk, k1, turn.

Row 4: Sl 1, p8, p2tog, p1, turn.

Row 5: Sl 1, k9, ssk, k1, turn.

Row 6: Sl 1, p10, p2tog, p1, turn.

Row 7: Sl 1, k11, ssk, k1, turn.

Row 8: Sl 1, p12, p2tog, p1, turn.

Row 9: Sl 1, k13, ssk, k1, turn.

Row 10: Sl 1, p14, p2tog, p1, turn.

Row 11: Sl 1, k15, ssk, k1, turn.

Row 12: Sl 1, p16, p2tog, p1, turn.

Row 13: Sl 1, k17, ssk, k1, turn.

Row 14: Sl 1, p18, p2tog, p1, turn.

Row 16: Sl 1, k19, ssk, turn.

Row 17: Sl 1, p19, p2tog, turn —21 sts rem.

Slip 40 instep sts onto one needle.

Foot

Gusset: K11 underheel sts, with empty needle k10 underheel sts and pick up and k18 sts along side of heel flap, pm, k40 instep sts, pm, with another empty needle pick up and k18 sts along other edge of heel flap then knit first 11 sts from underheel onto same needle—97 sts, pm of different color to indicate beg of rnds. Beg gusset shaping *and at the same time*, work in one rose across the instep, as appropriate. Strand yarns across back as necessary (fasten down later when darning in ends). Join in cir and beg rnds.

Rnd 1: Knit.

Rnd 2: On needle #1, knit to last 3 sts, k2tog, k1. With needle #2, k40 instep sts. With needle #3, k1, ssk, knit to end of rnd.

Rep these 2 rnds until 79 sts remain, dec one stitch from beg of rnd—78 sts. Now beg working back and forth in St st working three patterns across, up to the end of third repeat. Dec one st each end of instep sts on last row—76 sts.

Shape toe: Change to dpn and arrange sts thusly: 19 sts on needle #1, 38 sts on needle #2, and 19 sts on needle #3.

Rnd 1: On needle #1, k to last 3 sts, k2tog, k1. On needle #2, k1, ssk, k to last 3 sts, k2tog, k1. On needle #3, k1, ssk, k to end.

Rnd 2: Knit.

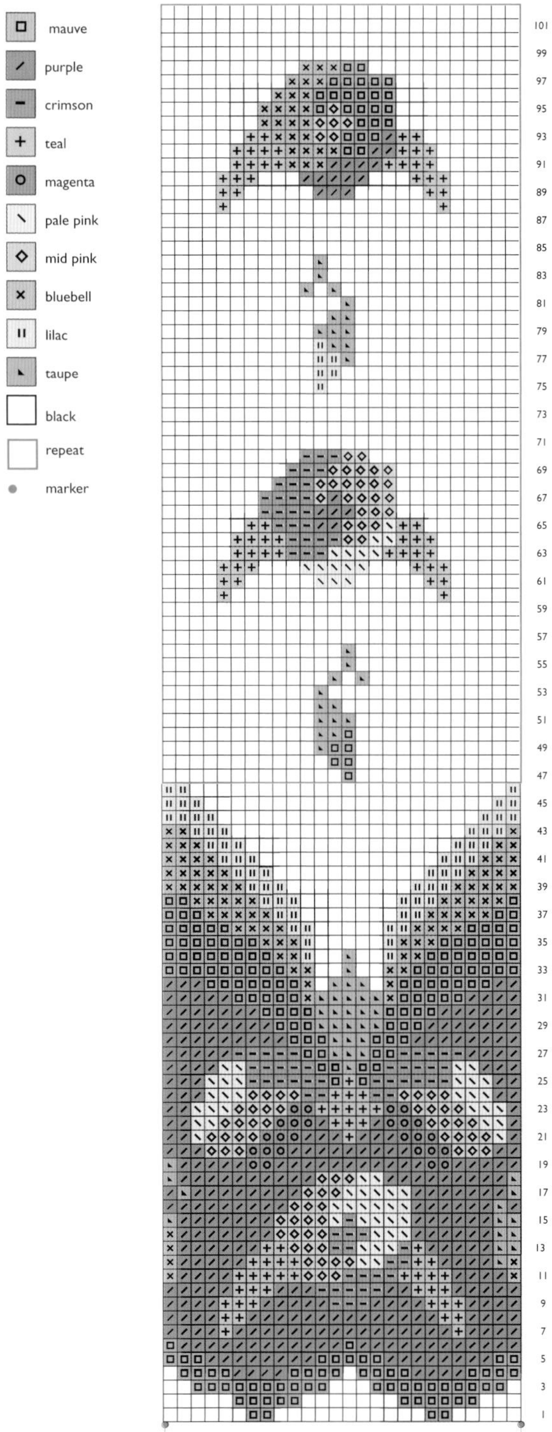

work patt multiple between markers 3 times—78 sts

Repeat these two rnds until 28 sts remain. K sts from needle #1 onto end of needle #3. Align two needles each with 14 sts and graft together using Kitchener stitch or 3-needle BO on the WS (see Glossary, page 9).

Finishing

Weave in all loose ends. With yarn threaded on a tapestry needle, sew instep seam and back leg seam.

Crochet Chain Arch Border:

Rnd 1: With MC and crochet hook and RS facing, join yarn to top of cuff. *Ch 5, sl st into 4th CO st along (after seaming back leg, you should have 76 CO sts in which to work) *; rep from * to * around top of cuff.

Rnd 2: Sl st into first 3 ch of previous row *ch 5, sl st into 3rd ch of next arch; rep from * around top of cuff.

Rnds 3, 4, and 5: Work as for rnd 2.

Rnd 6 ***(Picot Trim):*** *With MC sl st up first 3ch of previous row, ch 3, 1 sl st (into same st), 3 sl st; rep from * around top of cuff. Break yarn and pull through last st to secure. Weave in loose ends. Press lightly with a warm iron over a damp cloth.

Sasha Kagan is one of the world's best-known knitwear designers. She studied at the Royal College of Art in London; inspirations include the work of William Morris and her years as a costume designer for the-ater. Today she lives in rural Wales, where she creates new designs, characteristically elegant and colorful. She's authored several knitting books, and her work was recently the subject of an exhibition at London's Victoria and Albert Museum. "I am dedicated to promoting handknitting," Sasha says, "and a picture sent to me of one of my designs knit by a young person gives me a bigger thrill than a special commission."

SCANDINAVIAN STOCKING

Donna Kay

This beautiful, finely knitted cuffed stocking, which combines several different Scandinavian-inspired motifs, first appeared in Interweave Knits *magazine (Winter 99/00 issue). The knitting begins at the edge of the cuff. After the cuff is completed, turn it inside out and proceed with the leg and foot. When finished, the cuff folds over so that the right side is facing outward.*

Finished Size
About 7½" (19 cm) across top of stocking; 20" (51 cm) long.

Yarn
2 ply jumper weight yarn, approximately 450 yd (412 m) crimson; 300 yd (275 m) pine forest; 150 yd (137 m) yellow ochre.

Needles
Size 2 (2.5 mm): 16" (40 cm) circular (cir); size 0 (2 mm): 16" (40 cm) cir and set of 5 double-pointed (dpn). Adjust needle sizes if necessary to obtain the correct gauge.

Notions
Markers (m); tapestry needle.

Gauge
34 sts and 40 rows = 4" (10 cm) in color patt on larger needle; 34 sts and 46 rows = 4" (10 cm) in St st on smaller needle.

Note When working the checked purl pattern, remember to strand yarns not in use on the wrong side of the work.

Stitches

Checked purl stitch:
(multiple of 4 sts)

Rnd 1: *K2 with pine forest, k2 with crimson; rep from *.

Rnds 2 and 3: *P2 with pine forest, p2 with crimson; rep from *.

Rnd 4: *K2 with crimson, k2 with pine forest; rep from *.

Rnds 5 and 6: *P2 with crimson, p2 with pine forest; rep from *.

Rep Rnds 1–6 for patt.

Leg

Cuff: With pine forest and larger needle, CO 128 sts. Place marker (pm) and join, being careful not to twist sts. Purl 1 rnd. Join crimson and work Rows 1–45 of Cuff chart. Break off pine forest and turn cuff inside out. Change to smaller cir needle. Join crimson and with WS of cuff facing, cont until crimson section measures 3" (7.5 cm). ***Leg:*** Change to larger needle. Work Rows 1–50, then 1–31 of Leg chart. Break off crimson.

Heel

Sl the first 32 sts from left point of cir needle to right point (heel sts). Sl next 64 sts (instep sts) onto spare needle. ***Heel flap:*** (worked back and forth in rows) With RS facing, join pine forest and knit across the 64 heel sts. The m for the beg and end of rnds should be bet the 32nd and 33rd sts. Turn and knit back and, *at the same time*, inc 1 st at each end of needle—66 sts. Join crimson and work Rows 1–6 (back and forth) of Cuff

chart for a total of 30 rows. ***Turn heel:*** Cont in patt, shape heel as foll:

Row 1: Work to 2 sts before m, k2tog, sl m, k2tog, work to end of row.

Row 2: Work even in patt.

Rep Rows 1 and 2 five times more—54 sts rem; 42 rows of patt worked total. Break off crimson. Break off pine forest, leaving a 24" (61 cm) tail. Thread tail through tapestry needle and with RS facing, fold heel in half at m so that needles are held parallel with points facing to the right. Graft both sets of 27 sts tog using Kitchener stitch (see Glossary, page 9), removing m. ***Heel edging:*** With pine forest, pick up and knit 72 sts evenly spaced along open edge of heel sts, turn, and knit back.

Foot

Change to smaller cir needle. With RS facing, and beg at right corner of heel, sl the first 36 sts from the left needle point to the right point. Join crimson, pm, k36 heel sts, pm, k64 instep sts from spare needle, pm, knit rem 36 heel sts—136 sts.

Gusset:

Rnd 1: Sl m, knit to 3 sts from second m, k2tog, k1, sl m, k64, sl m, k1, ssk, knit to m.

Rnd 2: Knit.

Rep Rnds 1 and 2 seven times more—120 sts rem. Remove gusset markers. Work even until piece measures 5½" (13.5 cm) from heel. ***Shape toe:*** Break off crimson and join pine forest, working one rnd. Work Rows 1–3 of Leg chart, using pine forest as the background color. Change to dpn, placing 30 sts on each of 4 dpn (knit with the 5th dpn). Dec as foll:

Rnd 1: *K13, k2tog; rep from *.

Rnd 2 and all even-numbered rnds: Knit.

Rnd 3: *K12, k2tog; rep from *.

Rnd 5: *K11, k2 tog; rep from *.

Cont dec as established, working 1 less st before decs every other rnd until 8 sts rem. Break off yarn leaving an 8" (20.5 cm) tail. Thread tail on tapestry needle, draw through sts, and fasten off.

Finishing

Weave in loose ends. With damp cloth and iron, block to measurements, avoiding checked purl sts. ***Hanging loop:*** With pine forest and dpn, work 3-st I-cord (see Glossary, page 8) for 2½" (6.5 cm). Fold I-cord to make a loop and sew ends to top of cuff.

Donna Kay began knitting after graduating from college and has never looked back; her repertoire includes custom knitting, designing, and instructing. Traditional designs are her passion, especially colorwork. She's won several Best of Show awards, both regionally and nationally, and has designed for publications including Interweave Knits, Cast On *and* Knitting Now. *Donna knits in New Hampshire on the farm she shares with her husband and four children.*

- crimson
- ◆ pine forest
- × yellow ochre
- • Purl with appropriate color
- ② Yarn over 2 times with pine forest (drop second yarn over on next row)
- / K2tog with pine forest

Cuff

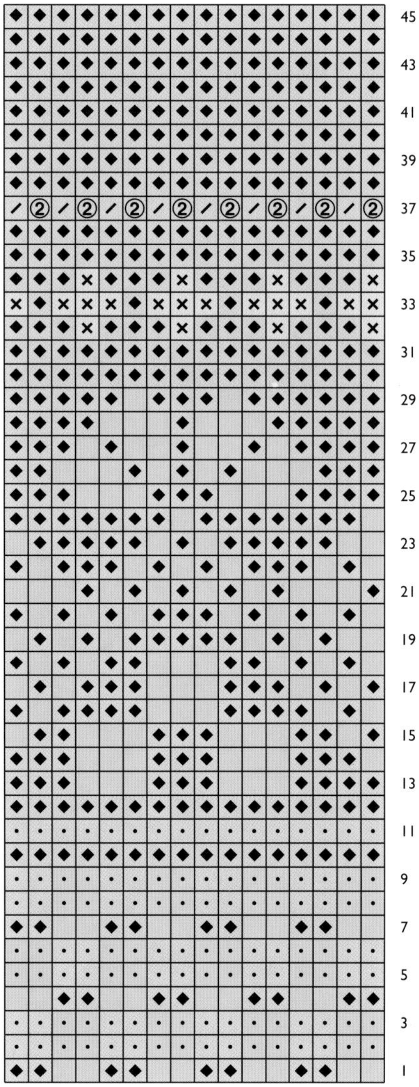

Leg

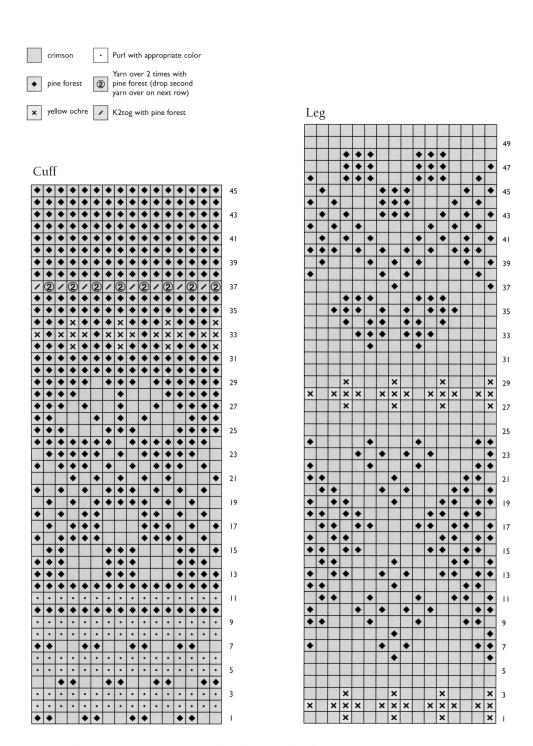

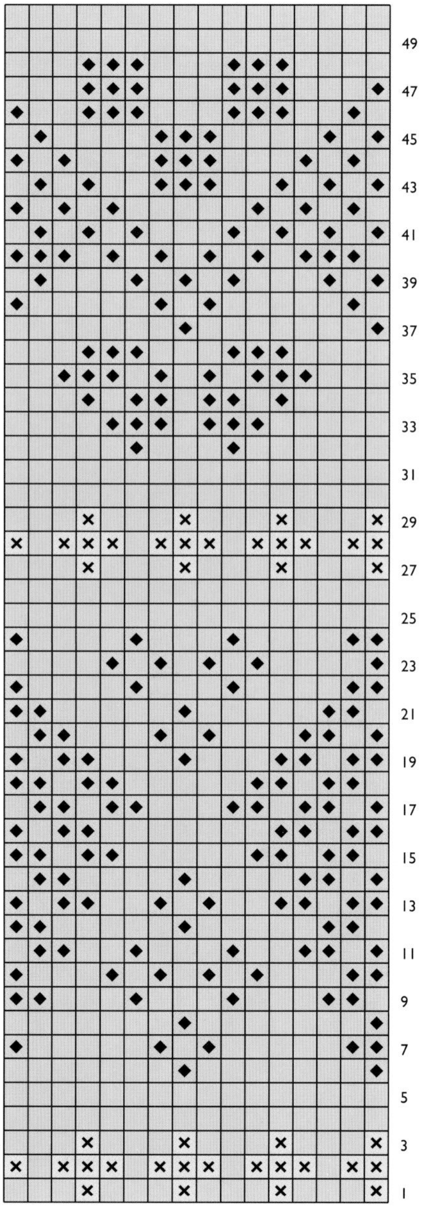

Scandinavian Stocking

CELTIC CHRISTMAS FAIR ISLE STOCKING

Ron Schweitzer

THE TRADITIONAL ENGLISH CHRISTMAS CAROL THE HOLLY AND THE IVY *INSPIRED RON SCHWEITZER'S FAIR ISLE DESIGN. "OF ALL THE TREES THAT ARE IN THE WOOD, THE HOLLY WEARS THE CROWN," GOES THE SONG, AND SO DEEP HOLLY GREEN CROWNS THE WINTERY TREE PATTERN OF THIS GENEROUSLY SIZED STOCKING.*

Finished Size
About 7" (18 cm) across top of stocking; about 24" (61 cm) from top to bottom.

Yarn
Double knitting weight yarn (color names in parentheses refer to the yarn used in photographed stocking; see yarn list for specifications): Approximately 130 yd (119 m) each deepest green (pine forest) and warm gray heather (fog); 85 yd (78 m) each dark green (bottle), teal green (eucalyptus), medium dark green (rosemary), sage green (sage), very light pink heather (sand), and warm shell heather (oyster); 5–10 yd (5–10 m) each red (crimson), white, light grayish blue heather (Highland mist), light violet heather (mist).

Needles
Size 6 (4 mm) and size 5 (3.75 mm): 16" (40 cm) circular or set of 5 double-pointed needles (dpn). Adjust needle size if necessary to obtain the correct gauge.

Notions
Markers (m); stitch holders; tapestry needle.

Gauge 28 sts and 28 rows = 4" (10 cm) with larger needles and chart B.

Notes The heel and toe are shaped using short rows. All sts are slipped purlwise. Yarn to front (YTF) or yarn to back (YTB) refers to the side of the work currently facing you, not the right side or wrong side of the work. Adjust the wraps so they are not too tight because they will be difficult to work off, especially on purl rows. See Glossary, page 8, for a guide to wrapping short rows. The back and forth row gauge in the toe and heel must match the cir, stranded gauge. Change needle size for toe and heel if necessary to match gauges.

LEG

Cuff: With deepest green (pine forest) and smaller needles, cast on 100 sts; if using dpn, distribute 25 sts on each needle. Place marker for beginning of rnd and join, being careful not to twist sts; purl one rnd. Work rnds 1–8 below; on rnds 2, 4, and 6, strand color not in use across the back of the work.

Rnd 1: *K1 red (crimson), k3 deepest green (pine forest), rep from * around.

Rnd 2: *P1 red, p3 deepest green, rep from * around.

Rnd 3: *K1 deepest green, k1 red, rep from * around.

Rnd 4: *P1 deepest green, p1 red, rep from * around.

Rnd 5: Rep rnd 1.

Rnd 6: Rep rnd 2.

Rnd 7: With deepest green, knit.

Rnd 8: With deepest green, purl.

Attaching and breaking off colors as needed, with larger needles work Rnds 1–15 of chart A. With smaller needles and deepest green, knit one rnd, purl one rnd; continuing with smaller needles, rep Rnds 1–8 above. With warm gray heather (fog), knit one rnd. ***Leg:*** Attaching and breaking off colors as needed, with larger needles work the 18 rnds of chart B 4 times until work measures about 14¼" (36 cm) from the beginning of the cuff, ending with rnd 18.

Heel

Sl next 25 sts from LN to RN; put the next 50 sts (instep sts) onto a holder. There should now be 50 sts on the working needle, with the beg of rnd marker between the 25th and 26th sts.

****Row 1:* Attach warm gray heather (fog) to the first st on the working needle; with smaller needles k49, sl next st to RN, YTF, turn, sl first st on LN to RN, YTF around slipped st and in position to purl the next st.

Row 2: P 48, sl next st to RN, YTB, turn, sl first st on LN to RN, YTB around slipped st and in position to knit the next st.

Row 3: K 47, sl and wrap next st as row 1.

Row 4: P 46, sl and wrap next st as row 2. Repeat rows 3 and 4 knitting or purling 1 st less each row until there are 30 unwrapped sts in the center of the heel (15 on each side of the beg of m) with 10 wrapped sts on each side of the 15 unwrapped sts.***

Turn heel:

Row 1: Knit across to first wrapped st. Insert needle under wrap, then into the st and knit the wrap and st together. Sl and wrap next st as row 1 above; notice that there are now 2 wraps on the st just turned.

Row 2: Purl across to first wrapped st. Insert needle from front to back under wrap, then into the st and purl the wrap and st together. Sl and wrap next st as row 2 above; notice that there are now 2 wraps on the st just turned.

Row 3: Knit across to the first double wrapped st. Insert needle under the 2 wraps then into the st and knit the wraps and st together. Sl and wrap next st as row 1 above.

Row 4: Purl across to the first double wrapped st. Insert needle from front to back under the 2 wraps

- ▲ dark green (bottle)
- \ teal green (eucalyptus)
- / warm gray heather (fog)
- × lt gray-blue heather (Highland mist)
- ıı lt violet heather (mist)
- ○ warm shell heather (oyster)
- ■ deepest green (pine forest)
- + med. dark green (rosemary)
- ◆ sage green (sage)
- □ lt pink heather (sand)
- ◇ white
- ● marker

Chart A—Cuff

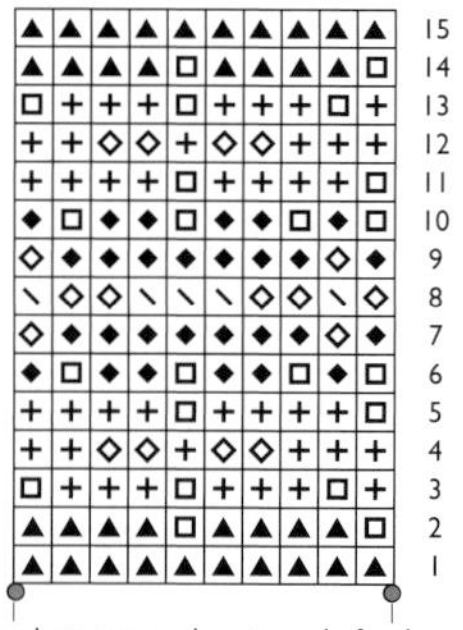

rep between markers to end of rnd.

Chart B—Leg & Foot

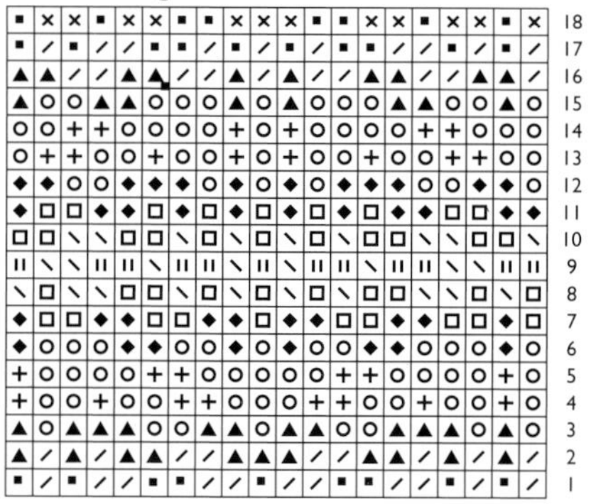

and into the st and purl the wraps and st together. Sl and wrap next st as row 2 above.

Repeat rows 3 and 4 until all wraps have been worked off. There are now 50 unwrapped sts on the working needle.

Foot

With left end of working needle, pick up the 50 sts on holder; sl next 25 heel sts to beg of rnd marker. Beg next rnd with the first st after the marker. Attaching and breaking off colors as needed, with larger needles beg rnd 1 of chart B and work the 18 rnds 3 times.

Toe

Sl next 25 sts from LN to RN, put next 50 sts on holder (toe top). On the 50 sts rem on the needle (toe bottom), work *** to *** of heel instructions. On next row, knit across to end of needle, working off all wraps. Turn work (without wrapping) and make a YO before working the first purl st. Purl across to the other end of needle working off all wraps. Put the 50 completed toe bottom sts on a holder; work the 50 sts of toe top exactly as for bottom. Join the top and bottom of toe using either Kitchener stitch or 3-needle bind-off for a firmer join (see Glossary, page 9). When joining, work the YO with its neighbor st.

Finishing

Weave in any loose ends. With tapestry needle and matching color, close any gaps created by stretched sts at the leg-heel-foot join and the foot-toe join. Wash and block to finished measurements. ***Hanging loop:*** With smaller needles and deepest green, work a 3-st I-cord (see Glossary, page 8) for 2½"–3" (6.5–8 cm). Fold I-cord in half and sew ends to starting edge of cuff.

A graphic designer, musician, photographer and writer as well as expert knitter, Ron Schweitzer began knitting on a dare from his wife and says he instantly had a sensation of "coming home." He describes each of his Fair Isle designs as "a unique expression of a feeling about an event, a place, or some remembered joy suspended in time waiting to be shared." Yarns International has published three collections of Ron's designs: Travel Logs *(1998),* Chesapeake Collection *(1999), and* Appalachian Portraits *(2000).*

AUSTRIAN ALPINE TREASURE

Candace Eisner Strick

THE TRADITIONAL AUSTRIAN TRAVELING-STITCH MOTIFS ON THIS STOCKING FOR EXPERIENCED KNITTERS SUGGEST A WINTERY DAY IN THE ALPS, SAYS DESIGNER CANDACE EISNER STRICK. THE SIDE PATTERNS ARE NAMED JAGERSTEIG, AFTER A NARROW UPHILL PATH USED BY HUNTERS. THE MIDDLE MOTIFS SUGGEST SNOWFLAKES AND TREES, AND THE NARROW PATTERNS ON EITHER SIDE OF THOSE ARE CALLED ALMWEG, OR ALPINE PATH. "AFTER THE MAIN LEG OF THE STOCKING IS COMPLETED, THE PATTERNS 'TRICKLE DOWN' LIKE A MOUNTAIN STREAM INTO THE FOOT, AND GRADUALLY DISAPPEAR," STRICK SAYS.

Finished Size
About 9" (23 cm) across top of stocking; 18½" (47 cm) from top to heel; 14" (35.5 cm) from heel to toe.

Yarn
Very tightly spun sport weight yarn, approximately 690 yd (630 m). Substitutions are not recommended for this stocking; see yarn information on page 95 for specifications.

Needles
Size 4 (3.5 mm): 16" (40 cm) circular and double-pointed (dpn). Adjust needle size if necessary to obtain the correct gauge.

Notions
Marker (m); tapestry needle.

Gauge
20 sts and 28 rows = 4" (10 cm) in St st. The traveling stitch patterns are somewhat stretchy, like ribbing, so gauge in patt st will not match the above gauge. Use the given gauge to help ascertain correct needle size for your knitting tension.

Note See "How to Work Traveling Stitches and Read the Charts" on page 81.

Leg

Border: With circular needles, CO 120 sts. Join, being careful not to twist sts, and place m for beginning of rnd. Knit 3 rnds for the hem. Work one rnd of *yo, k2tog* across rnd for picot turning. Knit 3 more rnds. Begin 20 sts repeat of pattern, making 6 points.

Rnd 1: *(P1, k1tbl) 4x, CD, (k1tbl, p1) 4x, yo, k1, yo; rep from * 6 times to end of rnd.

Rnd 2: *(P1, k1tbl) 3x, p1, CD, (p1, k1tbl) 3x, p1, yo, k3, yo; rep from * 6 times to end of rnd.

Rnd 3: *(P1, k1tbl) 3x, CD, (k1tbl, p1) 3x, yo, k5, yo; rep from * 6 times to end of rnd.

Rnd 4: *(P1, k1tbl) 2x, p1, CD, (p1, k1tbl) 2x, p1, yo, k7, yo; rep from * 6 times to end of rnd.

Rnd 5: *(P1, k1tbl) 2x, CD, (k1tbl, p1) 2x, yo, k9, yo; rep from * 6 times to end of rnd.

Rnd 6: *P1, k1tbl, p1, CD, p1, k1tbl, p1, yo, k11, yo; rep from * 6 times to end of rnd.

Rnd 7: *P1, k1tbl, CD, k1tbl, p1, yo, k13, yo; rep from * 6 times to end of rnd.

Rnd 8: *P1, CD, p1, yo, k15, yo; rep from * 6 times to end of rnd.

Rnd 9: Knit.

Rnd 10: Purl.

Increase rnd: (K6, M1) 20 times—140 sts.

Purl 1 rnd, knit 1 rnd, purl 1 rnd.

Begin Pattern: Follow chart 1 (Rnds 1–65 plus set-up rnd) across 70 sts for front of stocking, and repeating patt for other side. After completing Rnd 65, change to chart 2, working Rnds 1–34 of that chart. Cont to work the right and left side panels of chart 1 on either side of chart 2. When rep the right and left side patts, only work set-up rnd once, at the very beg of chart 1.

Heel

Heel flap: After the last rnd of chart 2 has been completed, break yarn. Put 26 sts from either side of marker on a dpn to work heel sts—52 sts. Leave the rem 88 sts of instep on circular needle. Attach yarn and work heel in the following patt:

Row 1: K3, work the stitches as they appear on the needle, either ktbl or p, to the last 3 sts, k2, slip the last stitch with yarn in front as if to purl.

Row 2: K3, work the stitches as they appear on the needle, working the purl stitches as purl tbl and the knit stitches as knit. Work the last 3 sts as k2, slip last stitch with yarn in front as if to purl.

Work above 2 rows 34 times (17 sl sts on outer edges of heel flap).

Turn heel:

Row 1: (RS) K26tbl to middle of row, k2tbl, sl 1, k1tbl, psso, k1tbl.

Row 2: Sl 1, p5tbl, p2tog, p1tbl.

Row 3: Sl 1, k6tbl, sl 1, k1tbl, psso, k1tbl.

Row 4: Sl 1, p7tbl, p2tog, p1tbl.

Row 5: Sl 1, k8tbl, sl 1, k1tbl, psso, k1tbl.

Cont as above, working one more stitch before the dec on each row, until all sts are worked—28 sts remain.

Foot

Gusset: K13tbl, with new dpn CD, k12tbl the next 13 sts of heel. Using the same needle, pick up and knit 17 sts along the heel flap. With a new

Sources: **The traditional Austrian designs were either taken directly or modified from *Bäuerliches Stricken,* by Lisl Fanderl (Rosenheimer, publisher); *Überlieferte Strickmuster aus dem Steirischen Ennstal,* by Maria Erlbach (Steiermärkisches Landesmuseum Joanneum Abteilung Schloss Trautenfels, publisher).**

needle, work the instep sts off the circular needle as follows: Ktbl for knit sts, purl for purl sts. (This is the same thing you did with the heel—working the sts as they appear on the needle.) With a new needle, pick up and knit 17 sts along other side of heel flap—148 sts, and with the same needle, k13tbl of heel sts. All sts for the bottom of the foot are now worked as ktbl. The instep sts are kept in the established patt, except for the following:

The middle sts of the leg that ended with a right twist (sts #20 and #21 on chart 2) on the last rnd of chart 2 are kept in this pattern, that is, turning them to the right every other row.

Now work the following two rnds 6 times:

Rnd 1: On needle #1, ktbl to last 3 sts, k2tog, k1tbl. On needle #2, p1, p2tog, work in pattern to last 3 sts, p2tog, p1. On needle #3, k1tbl, ssk, ktbl to end of needle.

Rnd 2: Work even in established pattern.

48 foot sts and 76 instep sts rem. Now work the foot even but decrease the instep sts (needle #2 **only**) as follows:

Rnd 1: P2tog at beg and end of instep sts—74 instep sts rem.

Rnd 2: P1, work the 2 sts of the twist, p2tog, work to 2 sts before next twist, p2tog, work the 2 sts of twist, p1—72 instep sts rem.

Work rnd 2 only six times—60 instep sts rem. Work even for 5 rnds. Continuing to work the foots sts even, work the following decreases on instep sts only:

Rnds 1 and 2: Work the first 5 sts, p2tog, work to 7 sts before end of instep sts, p2tog, work last 5 sts.

Rnds 3, 4, and 5: Work 7 sts, p2tog, work to 9 sts before end of instep sts, p2tog, work last 7 sts—50 instep sts rem.

Moving twists over instep sts: Continuing to work the sts of foot in ktbl, you will now start to move the 2 st twists over the instep sts on every rnd until they meet in the center of the instep sts.

Rnd 1: (instep sts only) P1, move the 2 sts of the twist one st to the left, working the st it passes over as ktbl. Move the 2 sts of the twist at the end of the instep sts one st to the right, working the st it passes over as ktbl. Cont to move these twists one st over on each rnd, always working the st it passes over as a ktbl. When they meet in the center of the instep sts, your instep sts will read on the needle as follows: p1, all ktbl until the center 4 sts that were the traveling twists, ktbl until one st from end, p1. From here on, all

- **b** — k1 tbl.
- right traveler: see accompanying article.
- left traveler; see accompanying article.
- purl on RS; knit on WS.
- patt repeat.
- marker.

Chart 1

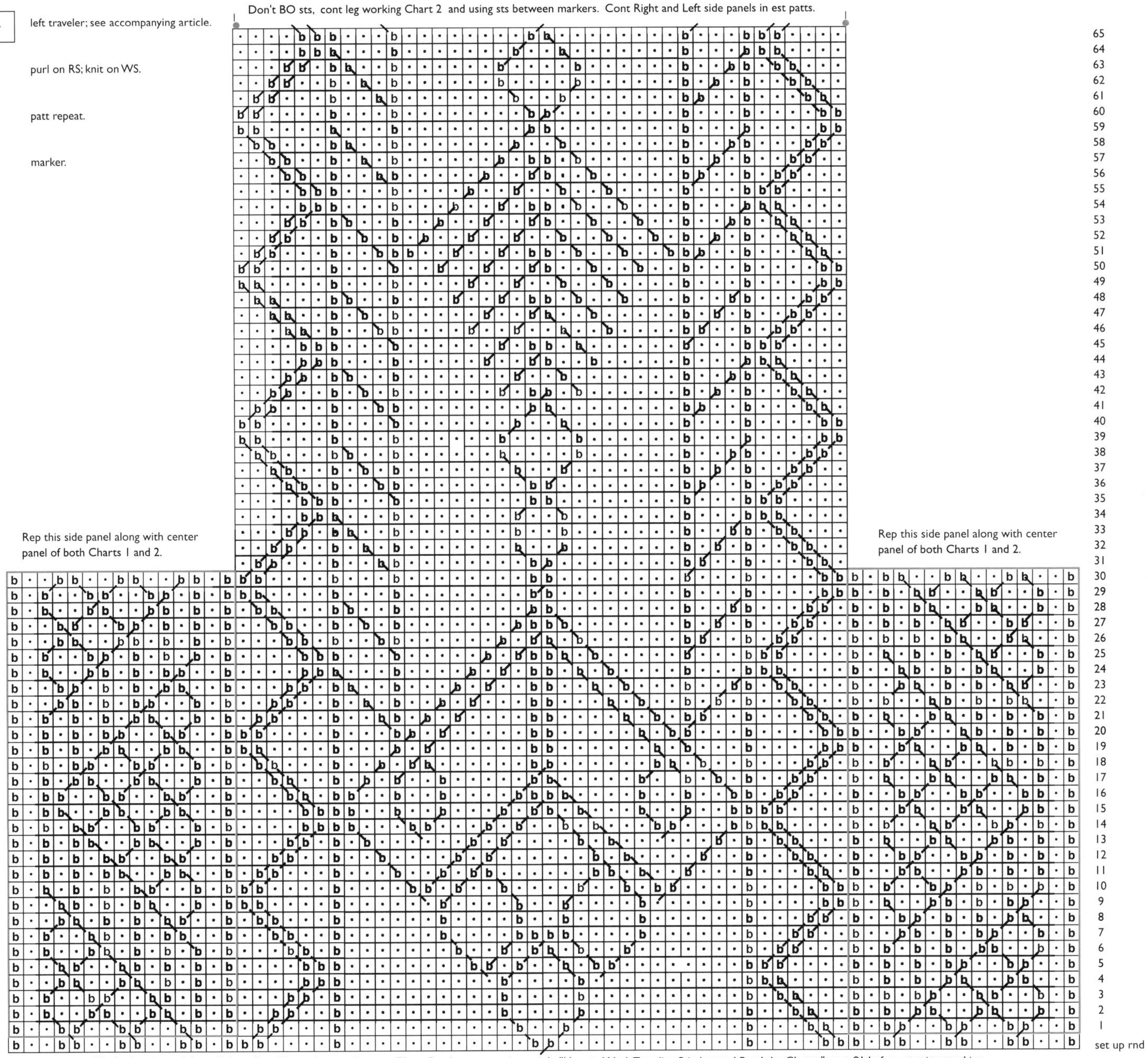

Don't BO sts, cont leg working Chart 2 and using sts between markers. Cont Right and Left side panels in est patts.
Rep this side panel along with center panel of both Charts 1 and 2.
Rep this side panel along with center panel of both Charts 1 and 2.
set up rnd

Work chart from right to left on first 70 sts, then rep for next 70 sts. Read accompanying article "How to Work Traveling Stitches and Read the Charts," page 81 before starting stocking.

Austrian Alpine Treasure

sts of instep are now worked as ktbl.

Next rnd: Work in all sts as ktbl, dec one st at beg of instep sts by working an ssk, and one st at end of instep sts by working k2tog—48 instep sts and 48 foot sts rem.

Toe

Rnd 1: On needle #1, ktbl to last 3 sts, k2tog, k1tbl. On needle #2, k1tbl, ssk, ktbl to last 3 sts, k2tog, k1tbl. On needle #3, k1tbl, ssk, ktbl to end of needle.

Rnd 2: Ktbl on all needles.

Rep these two rnds until 32 instep sts rem and 16 sts rem on each of needles #1 and #3. Now work rnd 1 only until 16 instep sts rem and 8 sts rem on each needles #1 and #3. Using needle #3, ktbl the sts from needle #1 so you have 16 sts on each of 2 needles. Carefully turn work inside out and do a three-needle bind-off (see Glossary, page 9).

Finishing

When blocking, do not press the traveling stitches. Instead, hover iron over stocking and use steam button, gently pulling the columns of pattern out. To block foot, because the ktbls tend to distort and make foot skew somewhat, gently mist and pin out on a carpet or board. Let dry overnight.

A knitter since the age of three, Candace Eisner Strick is the author of Sweaters from a New England Village *(Down East Books, 1996) and* Sweaters from New England Sheep Farms *(Down East Books, 2000). She teaches knitting at conventions and workshops around the country.*

Chart 2

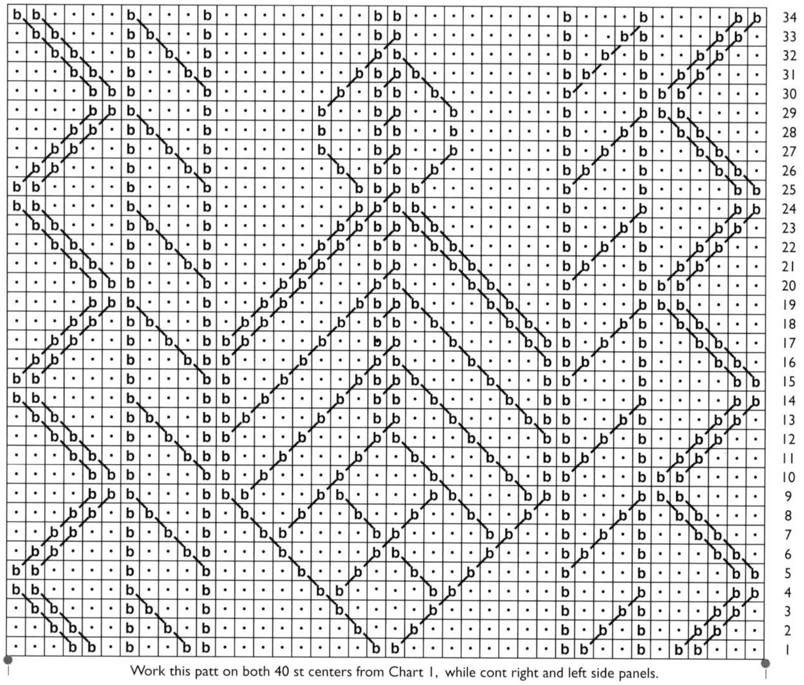

Work this patt on both 40 st centers from Chart 1, while cont right and left side panels.

How to Work Traveling Stitches and Read the Charts

Candace Eisner Strick

While these traveling stitches look rather complicated, they are actually quite simple to do with a little practice. Stitches are traveled by slipping them off the needle, exchanging places, and then working the designated stitch as either a knit or a purl.

- All knit stitches are worked as twisted stitches. If a knit stitch does not travel, it is worked by knitting through the back (abbreviated as ktbl—knit through back loop).
- Left travelers are twisted by knitting into the back of the stitch also. The stitches are first slipped as if to purl, places are exchanged, and then knit stitches are knit through the back.
- Right travelers become twisted stitches by the mere process of slipping them knitwise; this puts an automatic twist into the stitch. Once they have exchanged positions, they can then be worked the conventional way, i.e., through the fronts.
- Working the two methods in this slightly different manner makes the right and left traveling stitches perfect mirror images of each other.
- Note that slipping a purl stitch knitwise and then purling it the conventional way will make a twisted stitch. However, because it is tucked behind a knit stitch, it doesn't show.

Symbols

The "b" on the chart indicates a twisted stitch. All knit stitches are worked as twisted stitches, made by knitting into the back of the stitch if it is a left traveler and has been slipped purlwise, or by knitting into the front of the stitch if it is a right traveler and has been slipped knitwise. If this symbol appears but the stitch does not travel, it is executed by knitting through the back.

The dot (.) indicates a purl stitch.

Read all charts for traveling stitch patterns from right to left, bottom to top. These charts entail looking at two rows at once. The very first row is the set-up row; though generally worked without any stitches traveling, the middle two stitches of chart 1 in the Austrian Alpine Treasure pattern do entail a right traveler (see Example 1).

Once you've worked the set-up row, mark off the chart one row above this row, leaving the set-up row and row 1 visible. The set-up row is what now appears on your needle. Row 1 is what will appear on your needle after you've worked the slanted dash indications.

After completing row 1, mark off the chart so that now row 1 and row 2 appear. Row 1 is on the needle; row 2 will be on the needle after working the slanted dash indications.

Example 1

To work a right traveler (a knit crossing over a purl or a knit):

- Work to one stitch before the stitch with the slanted dash under it.
- Slip the next two stitches knitwise.
- With the left needle, go into the back of the first slipped stitch (this would be the second stitch from the tip on the right needle), pull the right needle out letting the knit stitch fall free in the front.
- Immediately pick it up with the right needle and put it back on the left needle.
- These two stitches have now exchanged places, but haven't been worked yet.
- Look up to the row in the chart and determine whether they will be worked as knits or purls. Since you have slipped the stitches as if to knit, the twist is already in the stitch, so knit through the front of the stitch and purl as usual. Usually the knit stays a knit and the purl stays a purl, but there are some exceptions to this rule, so always look first! See Example 1a in the sample chart, in

which the knit stays a knit, but the purl becomes a knit.

Example 2

To work a left traveler (a knit crossing over a purl or a knit):

- ❄ Work up to the knit stitch with the slanted dash under it.
- ❄ Slip the next two stitches purlwise.
- ❄ With the left needle go into the front of the knit stitch; pull the right needle out letting the other stitch fall free in the back.
- ❄ Immediately pick it up with the right needle and put it back on the left needle.
- ❄ These two stitches have now exchanged places, but haven't been worked yet.
- ❄ Look up to the row in the chart and determine whether they will be worked as knits or purls. Usually the knit stays a knit and the purl stays a purl, but there are some exceptions to this rule, so always look first! See example 2a in the sample chart, in which the knit stays a knit, but the purl becomes a knit. Since you've slipped the stitches as if to purl, you need to put the twist into the knit stitch by knitting into the back of the stitch.

Example 3

To work 2 right traveling knits over a purl or a knit:

- ❄ These stitches are indicated by two slanted dashes next to each other.
- ❄ Work up to the stitch before the first slanted dash.
- ❄ Slip this stitch, plus the 2 knit stitches with the dashes, all knitwise. With the left needle, go into the back of the first slipped stitch (this would be the third stitch from the tip of the right needle). Work as for Example 1, but crossing two knit stitches over one stitch.

Example 4

To work 2 left traveling knits over a purl or a knit:

- ❄ These stitches are indicated by two slanted dashes next to each other.
- ❄ Work up to the stitches with the first dash.
- ❄ Slip the two knit stitches with the dash plus the stitch after, all purlwise. With the left needle go into the fronts of the two knit stitches

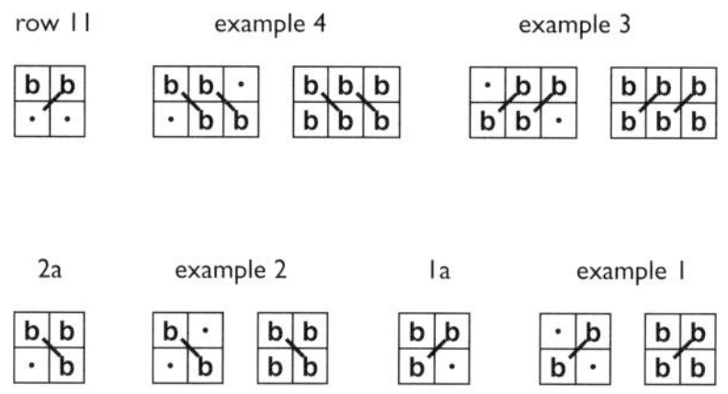

(these would be the second and third stitches from tip of right needle). Work as for Example 2, but crossing the two knit stitches over one stitch.

Special Indications for Austrian Alpine Treasure

Row 11, Chart 1, middle motif: Stitches #5 and #6 show a right traveling knit stitch over a knit stitch. However, on the needle they read as two purl stitches. Simply work the right traveler using the two purl stitches from the needle. When you are done executing the maneuver, they will now read on your needle as two knit stitches. Stitches #21 and #22 are worked the same way, but as left travelers.

Repeating a pattern: The two outermost side patterns of the stocking leg are written out only once. When the last round of the pattern has been completed, go back to the bottom of the chart and repeat the whole sequence. The stitches that are on the needle after the completion of the last row of the chart are what is indicated for the first row of the chart, or the set-up row. Do not work this row again, but rather work the traveling indications that are under the second row. When you are done working these indications, the stitches on your needle will now read what is indicated on row 2. Move your marker up one more row and continue working the repeat of the chart. ❄

MINIATURE MITTENS AND STOCKING ORNAMENTS

Barbara Albright

These charming miniature mittens and stockings are addictive to knit. Hang them on your Christmas tree, or make a festive chain of them to decorate any room in the house. Use them to hold gift cards on presents, or fill them with candies, chocolates, coins, messages, jewelry, or any tiny treasures.

Miniature Mittens

Note Add stripes or patterns as you wish; use repeating patterns between Rounds 17 and 28, where no shaping takes place, and center single motifs over the 12 stitches and 12 rounds that form the back of the hand. Instructions are given for working the nine-stitch thumbs as I-cord; while I-cord is easier than working so few stitches in the round on dpn, it does require pulling the yarn tightly at the beginning of each row to prevent loose stitches.

Mitten

Begin at cuff with smaller dpn, CO 24 sts. Arrange sts onto 3 dpn. Join, being careful not to twist sts.

Rnds 1-6: *K1, p1; rep from *.

Rnd 7: Change to larger dpn; knit, inc 1 st—25 sts.

Rnds 8, 10, 12, and 14: Knit.

Rnd 9: K12, M1, k1, M1, k12—27 sts.

Rnd 11: K12, M1, k3, M1, k12—29 sts.

Rnd 13: K12, M1, k5, M1, k12—31 sts.

Rnd 15: K12, M1, k7, M1, k12—33 sts.

Rnd 16: K12, place next 9 sts on a thread for thumb, k12—24 sts rem.

Rnds 17-28: Cont in St st.

Rnd 29: *K2tog, k2; rep from * to end of rnd—18 sts rem.

Rnds 30 and 32: Knit.

Miniature Mittens

Finished Size
Knit with fingering yarn, about 2" (5 cm) wide and 3½" (9 cm) long, including cuff. Use a heavier yarn for a slightly larger mitten.

Yarn
Fingering, sport, or double knitting yarn, approximately 15–20 yd (14–18 m).

Needles
Size 2 (2.75 mm): double-pointed needles (dpn); and size 3 (3.25 mm) dpn.

Notions
Tapestry needle; crochet hook (optional).

Gauge
Yarn shown has a gauge of 28 sts and 38 rows – 4" (10 cm) in St st on larger needles. Exact gauge is not important for this project, but will affect overall dimensions.

Rnd 31: *K2tog, k2; rep from * 3 times more, end rnd k2tog—13 sts.

Rnd 33: *K2tog; rep from * 5 times more, end k1—7 sts rem.

Cut yarn leaving a 6" (15 cm) tail. Thread tail on tapestry needle and draw through rem sts, pull tightly. Fasten off.

Thumb: Place 9 held thumb sts on larger dpn. Join yarn and knit 1 row. Work I-cord as foll: *Without turning needle, slide sts to right end of needle, pull yarn *firmly* around back to tighten, knit the 9 sts as usual. Rep from * 4 times more. *Next row:* *K2tog; rep from *, end k1—5 sts rem. Cut yarn, leaving a 6" (15 cm) tail. Thread tail on tapestry needle and draw through rem sts, pull tightly. Fasten off. Weave in loose ends. Tug on thumb to straighten loose stitches. ***Loop for hanging:*** Braid 3 strands of yarn or work single crochet for 3" to 4" (7.5 to 10 cm). Fold in half and sew inside cuff.

Miniature Stockings

Stitches

Seed Stitch:

Rnd 1: *K1, p1, rep from * around.

Following rows: K the purl sts and p the knit sts as they appear on the needle.

Leg

CO 24 sts. Arrange on 3 dpn and join, being careful not to twist sts. Work first 6 rnds in K1, p1 rib or in seed st. Work next 14-16 rnds in St st or until piece measures about 2" (5 cm) or desired length from beginning.

Heel

Heel flap: Change to contrasting color (CC) if desired. K first 12 sts onto needle #1. Arrange rem 12 sts evenly on needles #2 and #3. Work across on needle #1 for heel flap:

Row 1: Sl 1 purlwise, p11.

Row 2: Sl 1, k11.

Rep these two rows 3 times—8 rows.

Turn heel:

Row 1: Sl 1, p6, p2tog, p1, turn.

Row 2: Sl 1, k3, ssk, k1, turn.

Row 3: Sl 1, p4, p2tog, p1, turn.

Row 4: Sl 1, k5, ssk, k1—8 sts rem.

Foot

Gusset: Change back to main color (MC) if CC has been used. Continuing with same needle, pick up and knit 5 sts along left side of heel flap. With free needle, knit across 12 instep sts. With another free needle, pick up and knit 5 sts along right side of heel flap and first 4 sts of heel—30 sts. The beg of round is at center of heel. Knit 1 rnd.

Miniature Stockings

Finished Size

Knit with fingering yarn, about 2" (5 cm) wide at top, 3" (7.5 cm) top to heel, and 2½" (6.5 cm) heel to toe. Use a heavier yarn for a slightly larger mini-stocking.

Yarn

Fingering yarn, sport or worsted weight yarn, approximately 20-25 yd (18-23 m).

Needles

Size 2 (2.75 mm): double-pointed needles (dpn). If using heavier yarn, adjust needle size accordingly.

Notions

Tapestry needle; crochet hook (optional).

Gauge

Yarn shown has a gauge of 28 sts and 38 rows = 4" (10 cm) in St st. Exact gauge is not important for this project, but will affect overall dimensions.

Shape instep:

Rnd 1: On needle #1, k to last 3 sts on needle, k2tog, k1. On needle #2, knit across. On needle #3, k1, ssk, k to end.

Rnd 2: Knit.

Work above two rnds 3 times—24 sts rem. Knit 6-8 rnds or to desired length for foot. ***Shape toe:*** You should now have 6 sts on needle #1, 12 sts on needle #2, and 6 sts on needle #3. Change to CC if desired.

Rnd 1: On needle #1, k to last 3 sts, k2 tog, k1. On needle #2, k1, ssk, k to last 3 sts, k2tog, k1. On needle #3, k1, ssk, k to end.

Rnd 2: Knit.

Rep last 2 rnds 2 times more—12 st rem. *Next row:* On needle #1, k2tog, k1. On needle #2, k1, ssk, k2tog, k1. On needle #3, k1, ssk—8 sts rem. Knit 2 stitches from needle #1 onto needle #3.

FINISHING

With two needles holding 4 sts each, hold needles parallel, cut yarn with 12" (31 cm) tail, thread tail through tapestry needle and graft using Kitchener stitch (see Glossary, page 9). (If you prefer, instead of grafting sts, cut yarn, thread yarn on tapestry needle, pull needle through all sts and pull tightly; knot on inside.) Weave in ends. ***Loop for hanging:*** Braid 3 strands of yarn or work single crochet for 3" to 4" (7.5 to 10 cm). Fold in half and sew inside top of stocking (with cuff folded over if desired). Steam lightly if needed.

DESIGN YOUR OWN: BASIC STOCKING PATTERNS

Jean Lampe

JEAN LAMPE DESIGNED THESE LOVELY BASIC CHRISTMAS STOCKINGS, ONE EACH FOR SPORT/DOUBLE KNITTING, WORSTED AND BULKY WEIGHT YARNS, TO PROVIDE KNITTERS A CANVAS UPON WHICH TO EXPRESS THEIR CREATIVITY. THESE BASIC STOCKING INSTRUCTIONS CAN EASILY BE ADJUSTED TO SUIT WHATEVER MEASUREMENTS THE KNITTER CHOOSES.

We added duplicate stitch Santas (designed by Linda Ligon) and a simple border to the sport weight stocking. Jean added an easy purl-stitch Christmas tree to the worsted weight stocking, and knit the bulky-weight yarn stocking in bright colors and a rib pattern. We've included charts for the patterns shown, and an easy alphabet chart as a guide for adding a name, date, or message to these stockings (many other patterns in this book are also suitable for adding a name).

What will you do to personalize your stocking? Consider motifs in duplicate stitch or knitted-in using the intarsia method, embroidery, your favorite stitch patterns, or any other festive embellishments.

Basic Christmas Sock in Sport Weight/Double Knitting Weight Yarn

Note Slip markers each row or rnd for all stockings.

Leg

Using crochet chain method (see Glossary, page 8) provisionally CO 72 sts. Attach main yarn and knit all stitches, distributing evenly onto 4 dpn—18 sts each needle. Place m and join, being careful not to twist sts. Work 5 more rnds in St st. *Next rnd:* (picot edging) *k2tog, yo; rep from *. Cont in St st for 6 rnds. Fold hem to inside. Remove waste yarn placing live stitches on smaller size circ needle. *Next rnd:* Fuse hem to stocking by *inserting dpn tip into one stitch from stocking then one stitch from hem, k2tog; rep from * until all hem sts are joined to stocking. Work even on dpn until piece measures about 8½" (21.5 cm) or desired length from beg.

Heel

Heel flap: Work across 36 sts for heel, place next 36 sts on holder for instep. Work back and forth on heel sts as follows:

Row 1: (WS) Sl 1, p35.

*Row 2:**Sl 1, k1; rep from * to end of row.

Work last 2 rows 18 times (36 rows).

Turn heel:

Row 1: (WS) Sl 1, p24, p2tog, p1, turn.

Row 2: Sl 1, k15, ssk, k1, turn.

Row 3: Sl 1, p16, p2tog, p1, turn.

Row 4: Sl 1, k17, ssk, k1, turn.

Row 5: Sl 1, p18, p2tog, p1, turn.

Row 6: Sl 1, k19, ssk, k1, turn.

Row 7: Sl 1, p20, p2tog, p1, turn.

Row 8: Sl 1, k21, ssk, k1, turn.

Row 9: Sl 1, p22, p2tog, p1, turn.

Row 10: Sl 1, k23, ssk, k1. (26 heel sts)

Foot

Gusset: (RS) Slip last 13 under heel stitches onto empty needle. Using same needle, pick up and k18 sts along side of heel flap—31sts, pm, with empty needle, k36 of held instep sts, pm, with another empty dpn, pick up and k18 sts along other side of heel, plus knit the rem 13 under-heel sts from holding needle. Place marker using a different color to indicate beg of dec rnds. Work cir in rnds from this point.

Decrease row: *Knit to 3 sts before first m, k2tog, k1, knit across 18 instep sts, with empty needle knit rem 18 instep sts (instep sts are now divided onto two needles), slip m, k1, ssk, knit to end of rnd.

Rep from * for a total of 18 rnds —72 sts total. Remove markers except for m at beg of instep sts. Work even in St st until foot measures about 7½" (19 cm), or desired length from heel. Check to make sure each of the four dpn has 18 sts. Work to m before beg of instep sts (this marker indicates begin of rnds).

Shape toe:

Rnd 1: On needle #1, k2, ssk, knit rem sts on needle. On needle #2, knit to last 4sts, k2tog, k2. On needle #3, k2, ssk, knit to end of needle. On needle #4, knit to last 4 sts, k2tog, k2.

Rnd 2: Knit.

Work above two rnds 7 times—44 sts rem. Then rep rnd 1 every rnd 5 times—24 sts rem. Align sts onto two needles by slipping stitches from needle #2 onto needle #1, and stitches from needle #3 onto needle #4. You

Basic stockings (l to r): Worsted weight, sport/double knitting weight, and bulky weight yarns.

Basic Christmas Sock in Sport Weight/Double Knitting Weight Yarn

Finished Size

About 6" (15 cm) across top of stocking; 21" (53.5 cm) long.

Yarn

Sport weight or double knitting weight yarn, approximately 176 yd (161 m) pine green. For duplicate stitch Santas, small amounts each red, black, and tan sport weight yarn; small amount white angora or angora blend yarn.

Needles

Size 4 (3.5 mm): set of 5 double-pointed needles (dpn); smaller size 16" (40.5 mm) circ needle to hold cuff stitches. Adjust needle sizes if necessary to obtain the correct gauge.

Notions

Crochet hook; markers (m); stitch holder; tapestry needle. About 3 yds of smooth cotton waste yarn for provisional CO.

Gauge

24 sts and 32 rows = 4"(10 cm) in cir St st.

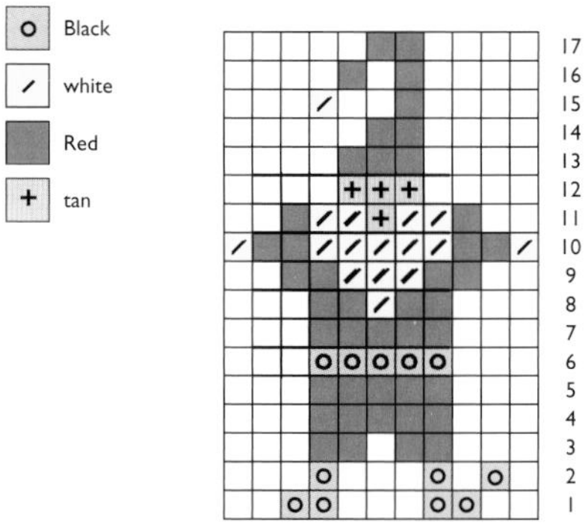

Santa

should now have 12 stitches from instep on needle #1 and 12 stitches from sole on needle #4.

Finishing

Cut yarn leaving about 18" (46 cm) tail for grafting. Thread yarn on tapestry needle and use Kitchener stitch (see Glossary, page 9) to graft sts. ***Finger Crochet hanger:*** Cut 2 yds (1.83 m) of yarn and make a finger crochet cord about 6" (15 cm) long, leaving two 4" (10 cm) yarn tails to attach cord to cuff hem. (I-cord, braid, or single crochet can also be used to make cord.) Fold cord in half, thread one yarn tail on tapestry needle and stitch cord to stocking, weave yarn end inside folded hem. Rep with other yarn tail to secure cord. Weave in loose ends. Block. ***Duplicate stitch Santas:*** Using tapestry needle and lengths of sport or double knitting weight yarn in black, red, and tan, and white angora or angora blend yarn, follow Santa chart using duplicate stitch (see Glossary, page 8). Place as desired. For border, work one duplicate stitch in red every 4th stitch around top of stocking and foot of stocking; work same in white a couple of rows below red, placing sts so they alternate with red stitches as shown.

Finger Crochet Hanger

Measure a length of yarn about nine times as long as the desired finished length. Make a slip knot at the halfway point. Insert your left index finger into the loop of the knot. Holding the knot between left thumb and middle finger, insert right index finger into the front of the loop, and draw through a new loop with End A. Hold knot lightly with right thumb and middle finger while you pull on End B to tighten up the first loop. Insert left index finger into front of loop, and draw through a new loop with End B. Hold the knot lightly with left thumb and middle finger while you pull on End A to tighten up the last loop. Cont in this manner until you reach yarn ends. Insert both ends though last loop and pull to tighten, then imbed ends through middle of chain to secure

Basic Christmas Sock in Worsted Weight Yarn

Notes Slip markers each rnd. In this stocking, the shaping takes place at the centers of both upper and lower foot (Double Decrease toe shaping) instead of the traditional side foot decreases. While this shaping would probably be uncomfortable in a wearable sock, it works quite well for a Christmas stocking, and provides an uninterrupted area for decoration along the entire foot, if desired.

Stitches

Seed Stitch:

Rnd 1: *K1, p1, rep from * around.

Rnd 2: Knit the purl stitches and purl the knit stitches as they appear on the needle.

Leg

Leaving a 2 yd (1.83 m) yarn tail, CO 60 sts. Place marker (pm) and join, being careful not to twist sts. Work in Seed st for 18 rnds, inc 2 sts evenly spaced on last rnd—62sts. Change to St st for 7 rnds then, if desired, follow chart working Christmas tree for 28 rnds. After completing chart continue working cir on 62 sts in St st until piece measures about 9½" to 10" (24 cm to 25.5 cm) from CO edge.

Heel

Heel flap: (worked back and forth in rows) Slip last 14 sts before m onto empty needle, knit first 14 sts after m and slip them onto the same needle—28 sts. Slip rem 34 sts onto spare needle or some smooth scrap yarn and hold aside for instep. Slip all edge stitches purlwise.

Row 1: (WS) Sl 1, p27.

Row 2: Sl 1, k27.

Rep these two rows for 20 rows.

Turn heel:

Row 1: (WS) Sl 1, p15, p2tog, p1, turn.

Row 2: Sl 1, k5, ssk, k1, turn.

Row 3: Sl 1, p6, p2tog, p1, turn.

Row 4: Sl 1, k7, ssk, k1, turn.

Row 5: Sl 1, p8, p2tog, p1, turn.

Row 6: Sl 1, k9, ssk, k1, turn.

Row 7: Sl 1, p10, p2tog, p1, turn.

Row 8: Sl 1, k11, ssk, k1, turn.

Row 9: Sl 1, p12, p2tog, p1, turn.

Row 10: Sl 1, k13, ssk, k1, turn.

Row 11: Sl 1, p14, p2tog, turn.

Row 12: Sl 1, k14, ssk—16 sts rem and RS is facing.

Foot

Gusset: Pick up and k12 sts along side edge of heel flap, pm, slip 34 instep sts onto 2 needles (17 sts each) and knit across both, pm, pick up and k12 sts along other side of heel flap, k8 sts from under heel, pm (use a different color marker here to indicate beg of rnd). Slip next 8 under heel sts onto first needle—74 sts.

Rnd 1: Knit to within 3 sts of first m, k2tog, k1, knit across 34 instep stitches to next marker, sl m, k1, ssk, knit to end of rnd.

Rnd 2: Knit one rnd.

Rep these two rnds until 64 sts rem (2 more sts than before heel). Remove all markers. ***Foot:*** Work even in St st until foot measures about 8" (20.5 cm). ***Double Decrease toe shaping:*** Place 32 instep sts on one dpn and 32 rem sts on another dpn. Locate the center sts and place a knitter's pin (or safety pin) in the 16th stitch on each needle to mark the center.

Rnd 1: Work even, arranging a few stitches from either end of the needles onto the other two dpns for ease in working rnds.

Rnd 2 (dec rnd): Work to 2 sts before marked stitch, slip 2 sts together (slip them as if you were going to work a k2tog), k1, p2sso—2 sts decreased. Knit around all sts until 2 sts before next marked stitch and work another decrease the same way.

Basic Christmas Sock in Worsted Weight Yarn

Finished Size
About 7" (18 cm) across top of stocking; 12" (30.5 cm) from top of stocking to heel; 10" (25.5 cm) from heel to longest section of toe.

Yarn
Worsted weight yarn, approximately 185 yd (170 m) Christmas red.

Needles
Size 7 (4.5 mm): set of 5 double-pointed needles (dpn) or 16" (40.5 cm) cir needle. Adjust needle size if necessary to obtain the correct gauge.

Notions
Markers (m); knitter's pin or safety pin; tapestry needle.

Gauge
20 sts and 24 rows = 4" (10 cm) in cir St st.

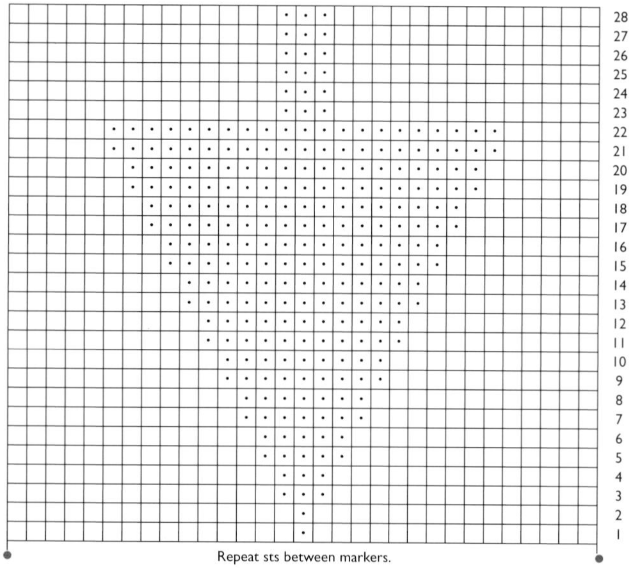

Christmas Tree

Rnd 3: Cont dec working up to one stitch before the last dec, then slip both sts together, knit the next st, p2sso. Work Rnd 3 until 20 sts rem. Align stitches on two needles, 10 on each.

Finishing

Close toe by grafting sts with Kitchener stitch (see Glossary, page 9). Weave in loose ends. ***I-Cord hanger:*** With dpn, CO 4 sts and knit I-cord (see Glossary, page 8) until about 8" (20.5 cm) long. Cut yarn leaving 6" tail. Thread tapestry needle with yarn and weave through I-cord sts, pulling gently to close. Imbed yarn through center of I-cord. Fold I-cord in half and attach securely to the back of the stocking. If desired, make a yarn "butterfly" with the yarn tail from CO, secure snuggly to the outside of stocking beneath attached I-cord. Weave in any loose ends.

Basic Christmas Sock in Bulky Weight Yarn

Leg

CO 60 sts. Place marker (pm) and join, being careful not to twist sts. Work in K4, p2 rib until stocking leg measures 8¼" (21 cm) or desired length.

Heel

Heel flap: (worked back and forth in rows) Slip 9 sts before and after m onto empty needle—18 sts. Knit across the last 9 slipped sts to bring working yarn to end of row. Place rem 42 sts on holder for instep. Slip all sts purlwise.

Row 1: Sl 1, p17.

Row 2: Sl 1, k17.

Rep above 2 rows 6 times for a total of 14 rows.

Turn heel:

Row 1: (WS) Sl 1, p11, p2tog, p1.

Row 2: Sl 1, k5, ssk, k1.

Row 3: Sl 1, p6, p2tog, p1.

Row 4: Sl 1, k7, ssk, k1.

Row 5: Sl 1, p8, p2tog, p1.

Row 6: Sl 1, k9, ssk, k1—12 sts rem, RS is facing.

Foot

Gusset: Pick up and k8 sts along side edge of heel flap, pick up and purl 2 sts slipping them onto the needle holding instep sts; work across rest of instep sts in established rib patt to m, pick up and k8 sts along other side of heel flap, k6 sts from under-heel, pm (use a different color marker here to indicate beg of rnd). Slip next 6 under heel sts onto first needle—72 sts.

Rnd 1: Knit to within 3 sts of first m, k2tog, k1, work across 44 instep stitches in est patt to next marker, sl m, k1, ssk, knit to end of rnd.

Rnd 2: Work even in est patts.

Rep above two rnds until 60 sts rem. Remove all markers, except m at beg of rnd. Cont in patts for another 3 rnds after dec rnds are completed. Join red and work 2 rnds. Work 4 rnds of blue. Join green and work 2 rnds. Work 7 rnds of blue and beg toe shaping.

Shape toe: (knit all stitches)

Rnd 1: *K2tog, k8; rep from * to end of rnd—54 sts.

Rnd 2: *K2tog, k7; rep from * to end of rnd—48 sts.

Rnd 3: *K2tog, k6; rep from * to end of rnd—42 sts.

Rnd 4: *K2tog, k5; rep from * to end of rnd—36 sts.

Rnd 5: *K2tog, k4; rep from * to end of rnd—30 sts.

Rnd 6: *K2tog, k3; rep from * to end of rnd—24 sts.

Rnd 7: *K2tog, k2; rep from * to end of rnd—18 sts.

Rnd 8: *K2tog, k1; rep from * to end of rnd—12 sts.

Cut yarn leaving about 8" (20.5 cm) tail. Thread tapestry needle and sew through rem 12 sts. Pull gently on yarn to close toe.

Finishing

Weave in loose ends on wrong side of work. ***Hanger:*** Cut 2 yd (1.83 m) lengths of yarn in each color. Working colors separately, make a finger crochet cord (see page 90) about 8" to 10" (20.5 cm to 25.5 cm) long. (I-cord, braid, or single crochet can also be used to make cord.) When all three cords are completed, braid together. Secure braid ends with sewing thread, fold braid in half and attach to inside of stocking top.

Jean Lampe is a free-lance technical editor, author, teacher, designer, and spinner. A frequently published author of technical articles, she is also a contributing editor for two national magazines and works as a technical editor for publishers and yarn companies. Her designs and articles have appeared in many magazines, booklets, knit and crochet kits, and television craft shows.

Basic Christmas Sock in Bulky Weight Yarn

Finished Size

About 5½" (14 cm) wide in rib patt; 16" (40.5 cm) long.

Yarn

Bulky weight yarn, approximately 150 yd (137 m) red (main color); about 6 to 8 yd (5.5 to 7.5 m) each royal blue and green (contrast colors) for stripes and hanger braid.

Needles

Size 10 (6.0 mm): set of 5 double-pointed needles (dpn) or 16" (40.5 cm) cir needle. Adjust needle size if necessary to obtain the correct gauge.

Notions

Markers (m); tapestry needle.

Gauge

14 sts and 18 rows = 4" (10 cm) in rib patt and St st.

Knitter's Alphabet

Use these simple, easy-to-read letters and numbers to add a name, date, or message, as shown above, to your Christmas stockings.

	x			x	x	x				x	x	x		x	x	x			x	x	x
x		x		x			x		x					x			x		x		
x	x	x		x	x	x			x					x			x		x	x	
x		x		x			x		x					x			x		x		
x		x		x	x	x				x	x	x		x	x	x			x	x	x
x	x	x			x	x	x		x		x		x			x	x	x			
x				x					x		x		x				x				
x	x			x		x	x		x	x	x		x				x				
x				x			x		x		x		x		x		x				
x					x	x			x		x		x			x					
x			x		x				x				x		x			x			
x		x			x				x	x		x	x		x	x		x			
x	x				x				x		x		x		x		x	x			
x		x			x				x				x		x			x			
x			x		x	x	x		x				x		x			x			
	x	x			x	x	x			x	x				x	x	x	x			
x			x		x		x		x			x			x			x			
x			x		x	x	x		x			x			x	x	x				
x			x		x				x			x			x			x			
	x	x			x					x	x		x		x			x			
x	x	x		x	x	x	x	x		x			x		x				x		
x						x				x			x		x				x		
x	x	x				x				x			x		x				x		
		x				x				x			x			x		x			
x	x	x				x					x	x					x				
x				x		x		x		x		x		x	x	x	x				
x		x		x		x		x		x		x				x					
x		x		x			x			x		x			x						
x		x		x		x		x			x			x							
	x		x			x		x			x			x	x	x	x				
x			x	x			x	x	x		x						x	x	x		
x		x			x				x		x		x				x				
x				x				x			x		x					x	x		
x			x						x		x	x	x	x		x			x		
x		x	x	x	x		x	x					x				x	x			
x				x	x	x	x		x	x	x		x	x	x			x			
x							x		x		x		x		x		x		x		
x	x	x				x				x			x	x	x		x		x		
x		x			x				x		x				x		x		x		
x	x	x		x					x	x	x				x			x			

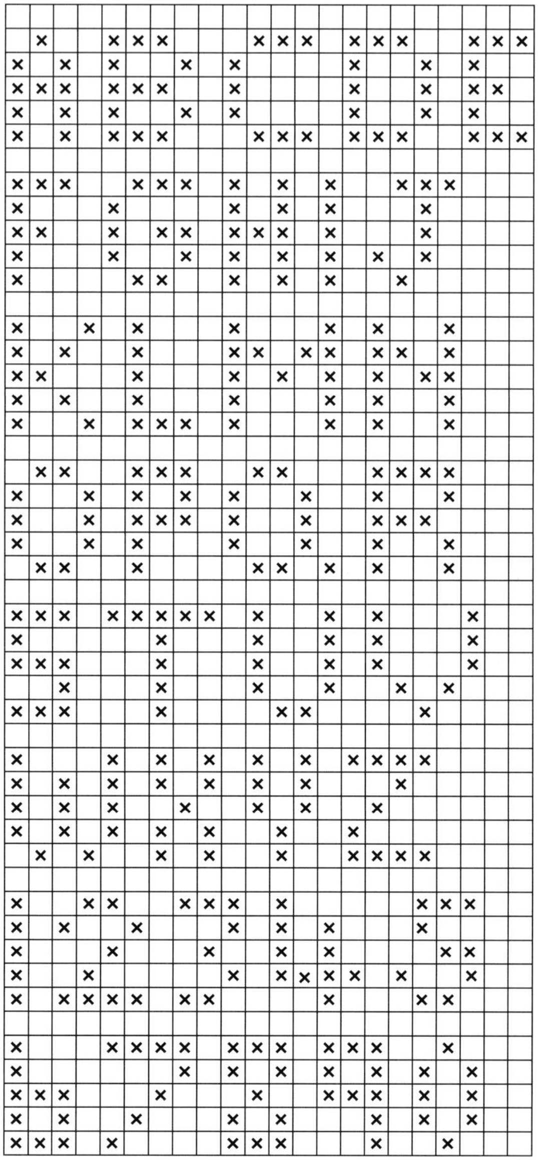

YARNS

Following are the specifications for the yarns our designers chose, as shown in the photographed stockings; most are widely available through local yarn retailers. Generic yarn weights and approximate yardages are provided in the patterns so you can easily make substitutions. See Yarn Suppliers, page 96, for information on contacting yarn companies listed.

Snowy Night Gansey Stocking
Knit One Crochet Too (K1C2) Parfait Solids (100% wool, 218 yd [200 m]/100g): 2 skeins #1590 sage green.

Christmas Rainbow Surprise
Noro Kureyon (100% wool, 109 yd [100 m]/50 g): 3 skeins #58 variegated.

Sock Monkey Stocking
Reynolds Candide (100% wool, 194 yd [178 m]/4 oz): 1 skein each #2 sheep gray, #7 scarlet, #6 washed white.

The Chubby Sock
Cascade 220 (100% wool, 220 yd [201 m]/100g): 1 skein each #8010 ecru, #8267 medium green, #9405 dark green, #9404 berry.

Paintbox Pocket Stocking
Harrisville Designs Highland Style (100% wool; 200 yd [183 m]/100g): 2 skeins #8 hemlock; small amounts each #40 topaz, #4 gold, #35 chianti, #30 azure, #47 suede.

The Big Easy
Classic Elite Yarns Waterspun Weekend (felted 100% merino wool, 57 yd [52 m]/100 g): 1 skein each #7268 madder, #7216 natural, #7215 dark green.

Keepsake Baby Stocking
Muench Yarns Touch Me chenille yarn (72% viscose, 28% wool, 60 yd [54 m]/ 50g): 1 skein each #3626 sky blue and #3621 teal. Muench Yarns Relax (10% alpaca, 32% wool, 32% nylon, 26% acrylic, 121 yd [110m]/ 50 g): 1 skein #4 natural.

Rowan Yarns Lurex DK (75% viscose, 25% lurex, 62 yd [57m]/25 g): small amount #842 gold.

Giant Jester Stocking
Brown Sheep Lamb's Pride Worsted (85% wool, 15% mohair; 190 yd [173 m]/4 oz [113g]; 1 skein each #M65 sapphire, #M145 spice, #M78 aztec turquoise, #M78 limeade.

Snowman at Midnight
Rowan Magpie (100% wool, 185 yd [169 m]/100g): 1 skein each #778 harbour blue, #002 natural, #684 berry; small amounts each #062 raven black and #766 sienna (orange).

Diamonds in the Rough Argyle Stocking
Tahki Donegal Tweed (100% Wool, 183 yd [167 m]/100g): 1 skein each #819 gray, #863 red, #878 green; small amounts #862 blue and #893 gold.

Village of Kirbla Estonian Stocking
Dale of Norway Heilo (100% wool, 108 yd [100m]/100g): 2 skeins #8972 dark green; 1 skein each #0020 natural, #9335 apple green, #9834 gold.

A Fetching Stocking
Mission Falls 1824 Wool (100% merino wool superwash; 85 yd [78 m]/1.75 oz [50g]); 2 skeins each #010 russet and #006 oatmeal; 1 skein each #016 thyme and #008 earth.

Counterpane and Lace Stocking
Classic Elite Mistral (85% pima cotton, 15% alpaca; 115 yd [105 m]/50g): 2 skeins #1355 autumnal red; 1 skein #1386 parchment.

Hugs and Kisses Aran Stocking
Berroco Wensleydale Longwool (100% wool, 174 yd [161 m]/100g): 2 skeins #101 white, 1 skein #140 dark olive.

Naughty but Nice Victorian Elegance
Jamieson & Smith Shetland 2 ply jumper weight (100% wool, 140 yd [128 m]/30g): 2 skeins #77 black; 1 skein each #120 taupe, #49 lilac, #131 bluebell, #FC74 magenta, #136 pale pink, #FC22 mid pink, #43 crimson, #141 teal, #44 mauve, #20 purple. (Only small amounts of some colors are used; see pattern instructions.)

Scandinavian Stocking
Jamieson's Naturally Shetland Spindrift 2 ply jumper weight (100% Shetland wool, 150 yd [137 m]/1 oz): 3 skeins #525 crimson, 2 skeins #292 pine forest, 1 skein #230 yellow ochre.

Celtic Christmas Fair Isle Stocking
Jamieson's Naturally Shetland Double Knitting (100% Shetland wool, 170 yd [155 m]/2 oz). One skein each #820 bottle; #525 crimson; #794 eucalyptus; #272 fog; #1390 Highland mist; #180 mist; #290 oyster; #292 pine forest; #821 rosemary; #766 sage; #183 sand; #304 white. (Only small amounts of some colors are used; see pattern instructions.)

Austrian Alpine Treasure
Rauma 3tr. Strikke-garn (100% wool, 115 yd [105 m]/50g), #101 white, 6 skeins. Available in the United States from Arnhild's Knitting Studio (see Suppliers).

Mini-Stocking and Mini-Mitten Ornaments
Zitron Libero (80% wool, 20% nylon, 164 yd [150 m]/50g): 1 skein #150 variegated (will make several ornaments).

Patons Kroy (85% washable wool, 15% nylon, 203 yd [186 m]/50g): #437 geranium, small amount used for ornaments shown.

Dale of Norway Baby (100% washable merino wool, 191 yd [175 m]/50g): #7854 forest green, small amount used for ornaments shown.

Basic Christmas Sock, Sport/DK Weight
Knit One Crochet Too Creme Brulee (100% merino wool, 131 yd [120 m]/50g): 2 skeins #557 pine.

Embroidered Santas:
Brown Sheep Nature Spun sport weight yarn (100% wool, 184 yd [168 m]/50 g): small amounts #N12 Sahara tan, #N46 red fox, #601 pepper black.

Tahki Jolie (70% French angora, 30% merino wool, 108 yd [99 m]/25g): small amounts #5001 natural.

Basic Christmas Sock, Worsted Weight
Plymouth Encore (75% acrylic, 25% wool, 200 yd [183 m]/100g): 1 skein #1386 Christmas red.

Basic Christmas Sock, Bulky Weight
Baabajoe's Wool Pak Yarns NZ (100% wool, 310 yd [284 m]/250g). 1 skein #34 royal blue; small amounts #36 royal red and #37 royal green.

YARN SUPPLIERS

Baabajoes Wool Company
www.baabajoeswool.com
PO Box 260604
Lakewood, CO 80226

Berroco Yarns
Info@berroco.com
PO Box 367
Uxbridge, MA 01569-0367
(800) 343-4948

Brown Sheep Yarns
www.brownsheep.com
100662 County Road 16
Mitchell, NE 69357
(308) 635-2198

Cascade Yarns
www.cascadeyarns.com
PO Box 58168
Tukwila, WA 98138
(206) 574-0440

Classic Elite Yarns
300 Jackson St.
Lowell, MA 01852
(800) 343-0308

Dale of Norway Yarns
www.dale.no
N16 W23390 Stoneridge Dr., Ste. A
Waukesha, WI 53188
(800) 441-3453

Harrisville Yarns
www.harrisville.com
PO Box 806, Center Village
Harrisville, NH 03450
(800) 338-9415

Jameison & Smith Shetland
U.S. Distribution: School House Press
6899 Cary Bluff
Pittsville, WI 54466
(715) 884-2799

Jamieson's Naturally Shetland
U.S. Distribution: Unicorn Books and Crafts
unicorn@unicornbooks.com
1338 Ross St.
Petaluma, CA 94954
(707) 762-3362

Knit One Crochet Too Yarns
K1C2 Solutions
k1c2@ix.netcom.com
2220 Eastman Ave., #105
Ventura, CA 93003
(800) 607-2462

Mission Falls Yarns
U.S. Distribution: Unique Kolours
www.uniquekolours.com
1428 Oak Ln.
Downingtown, PA 19335
(800) 252-3934

Muench Yarns
Muench/GGH
muenchyarns@aol.com
285 Bel Marin Keys Blvd., Unit J
Novato, CA 94949-5724
(415) 883-6375

Noro Yarns
U.S. Distribution: Knitting Fever Inc.
www.knittingfever.com
35 Debevoise Ave.
Roosevelt, NY 11575
(800) 645-3457

Patons Yarns
www.patonsyarns.com
100 Sonwil Dr.
Buffalo, NY 14225

Plymouth Yarns
www.plymouthyarn.com
PO Box 28
Bristol, PA 19007
(800) 523-8932

Rauma Yarns
U.S. Distribution: Arnhild's Knitting Studio
www.arnhild.com
2315 Buchanan Dr.
Ames, IA 50010-5370
(515) 232-7661

Reynolds Yarns/JCA
35 Scales Ln.
Townsend, MA 01469-1094
(800) 225-6340

Rowan Yarns
U.S. Distribution: Westminster Fibers
wfibers@aol.com
5 Northern Blvd.
Amherst, NH 03031
(603) 886-5041

Tahki Yarns
www.tahki.com
1059 Manhattan Ave.
Brooklyn, NY 11222
(800) 338-9276

Skacel Collection
www.skacelknitting.com
PO Box 88110
Seattle, WA 98138-2110
(800) 255-1278

Miscellaneous Suppliers

Sock Monkey Toy Socks and Instructions
Vermont Country Store sells the red-heeled cotton work socks used to make classic sock monkey toys. Sewing instructions for the monkey come with the socks.

Vermont Country Store
www.vermontcountrystore.com
PO Box 3000
Manchester Center, VT 05255-3000
(802) 362-8460

Notions Kit for Keepsake Baby Stocking
Contact Sophie's Yarns in Philadelphia, Pennsylvania to order a notions kit for the Keepsake Baby Stocking, including bells, ribbon, sequins, and acetate.

Sophie's Yarns
www.sophiesyarns.com
2017 Locust St.
Philadelphia, PA
(215) 977-9276